ASEAN

·本教材为广西旅游管理一流学科（培育）建设项目成果·

东盟英语新闻选读

Selected ASEAN English News Readings

主　编　◎张海琳　肖飞菲
副主编　◎徐　闻　杨文燕　谢琳琳　黄　艳
参　编　◎李　卉　冉　芳　李　莎　黄　倩

华中科技大学出版社
http://www.hustp.com
中国·武汉

内 容 简 介

东盟位于世界地理要冲,现有10个成员国,总面积约449万平方公里,人口6.49亿(截至2018年),文化形态丰富多彩而又独具特色,同时东盟又是一个多民族地区以及东西方文明交汇之所。中国与大多数东盟国家交往历史源远流长,在各领域开展全面合作,特别是2020年以来,东盟和中国已成为彼此最为重要的经贸、文化和旅游交流合作伙伴。

本书以英语新闻作为媒介,解读世界各国主要报刊、网站等各种媒体关于东盟各国的英文新闻报道,透过字里行间蕴涵的各种信息,管窥东盟社会、经济及文化等领域的最新发展,涉及时政、财经、社会、科技、教育、文化、环境、旅游等多个方面,旨在为读者提供一把了解东盟时事与文化的钥匙。全书按主题分为9个单元,每单元包括3篇新闻,每篇新闻附背景知识介绍,词汇和重难点句子解析,并配有阅读理解题和思考题。此外,为方便使用,本教材附有练习参考答案。所选阅读新闻均来自近年来原版英文报纸杂志,旨在提高学生的英语语言知识,如新闻词汇、句法、语篇等特点,开拓国际视野。本书适用大中专院校中级水平的非英语专业学习者,英语专业低年级学习者,以及大学英语四、六级,研究生入学考试等备考使用。

本书编写过程得到了桂林旅游学院东盟旅游研究基地和桂林理工大学外国语学院领导和同行的鼎力支持,在此表示衷心的感谢。由于时间仓促以及编撰者水平所限,书中难免有错谬之处,敬请广大读者批评指正。

图书在版编目(CIP)数据

东盟英语新闻选读/张海琳,肖飞菲主编.—武汉:华中科技大学出版社,2021.3
ISBN 978-7-5680-6929-8

Ⅰ.①东… Ⅱ.①张… ②肖… Ⅲ.①新闻-英语-教材 Ⅳ.①G210

中国版本图书馆CIP数据核字(2021)第040308号

东盟英语新闻选读 　　　　　　　　　　　　　　　张海琳　肖飞菲　主编
Dongmeng Yingyu Xinwen Xuandu

策划编辑:	王　乾
责任编辑:	倪　梦　王　乾
封面设计:	原色设计
责任校对:	李　弋
责任监印:	周治超
出版发行:	华中科技大学出版社(中国·武汉)　　电话:(027)81321913
	武汉市东湖新技术开发区华工科技园　　邮编:430223
录　　排:	华中科技大学惠友文印中心
印　　刷:	武汉科源印刷设计有限公司
开　　本:	787mm×1092mm　1/16
印　　张:	10.5
字　　数:	245千字
版　　次:	2021年3月第1版第1次印刷
定　　价:	49.80元

本书若有印装质量问题,请向出版社营销中心调换
全国免费服务热线:400-6679-118　竭诚为您服务
版权所有　侵权必究

前言
Preface

  东盟位于世界地理要冲。无论对于亚洲还是世界而言,东盟都是一个重要的地区,其文化形态丰富多彩而又独具特色,同时东盟又是一个典型的多民族地区,以及东西方文明的交汇之处。本书通过借用英语新闻作为媒介,解读世界各国报刊、网站等各种媒体关于东盟各国的英文主题的新闻报道(文章),透过字里行间所蕴含的各种信息,简要地了解东盟社会、经济及文化等领域的最新发展动态。本书涉及东盟的时政、财经、社会、科技、教育、文化、环境、旅游八个方面,旨在通过英语新闻为读者提供一把了解东盟时事与文化的钥匙。

  本书编写采用的是"以读新闻促思考"的理念,即在阅读新闻的基础上管窥和思考东盟国家的社会各方面。本书按主题分为9个单元,每单元包括3篇新闻,每篇新闻附背景知识介绍、词汇和重难点句子解析,并配有阅读理解题、思考探讨题和词汇题。此外,为方便大家使用,本书附有练习参考答案。本书所选阅读新闻均来自近年来原版英文报纸杂志,旨在提高学生的英语语言知识,如新闻词汇、句法、语篇等特点,培养学生直观性和客观性区别判断的能力。本书适用于大中专院校中级英语水平的非英语专业学习者,英语专业低年级学习者,以及大学英语四、六级,研究生入学考试及各类考生备考使用。

  本书撰写过程中坚持新闻学、翻译学及社会学等学科的交叉,从个案到整体,从微观到宏观,力求搜集最新的资料,获取更多的资讯,注重新闻主题和叙事的阐释分析,希望给读者带来更丰富的启发与思考。囿于作者的水平,谬误之处在所难免,敬希广大专家及读者给予批评与指正,不胜感激。本书撰写过程中得到了桂林理工大学外国语学院的许多专家、学者的宝贵意见与悉心指导,在此一并表达深深的谢意。

编者

目录
Contents

Chapter 1　Overview 概况

Reading 1　An Overview of ASEAN
东盟概况 /3

Reading 2　ASEAN Pledges to Ensure Food Security during COVID-19 Outbreak
东盟承诺在 COVID-19 疫情期间确保粮食安全 /6

Reading 3　ASEAN Holds Dialogue on the Rights of Persons with Disabilities
东盟举行讨论残疾人权利对话 /9

Chapter 2　Current Politics 时政

Reading 1　Indonesia will build its new capital city in Borneo as Jakarta sinks into the Java Sea
印尼总统决定迁都 /15

Reading 2　Gov't looking to strengthen laws on data protection
修正法案促网络安全 /19

Reading 3　Philippines passes law requiring students to plant 10 trees before graduating
菲律宾新法案：想毕业，先种树 /22

Chapter 3　Economy 经济

Reading 1　Southeast Asia's Leaders Call for Faster Asian Economic Integration
东南亚领导人敦促加快地区经济整合 /29

Reading 2　Singapore Monetary, Fiscal Policy "Appropriate" for Now：MAS
新加坡金融管理局：现在执行"恰当的"新加坡金融与财政政策 /32

	Reading 3	Vietnam Passes Cybersecurity Law Despite Privacy Concerns
/36		撇开隐私顾虑,越南通过网络安全法案

Chapter 4 Society 社会

/43	Reading 1	Man arrested in Singapore Changi Airport for buying ticket just to wave his wife off at the gate 男子在新加坡樟宜机场被捕,只因买机票送妻子到登机口
/46	Reading 2	Trash for tickets on Indonesia's "plastic bus" 回收垃圾出奇招:印度尼西亚推出"塑料公交车"
/50	Reading 3	Smoking inside a house equals to "domestic violence" 泰国控烟出新招 在家吸烟将视作"家暴"

Chapter 5 Science and Technology 科学和技术

/57	Reading 1	5G takes centre stage with various tech demos 各种5G技术演示成为瞩目焦点
/60	Reading 2	2020 Budget: A boost for Malaysia's tech industry 2020年预算:推动马来西亚科技产业发展
/65	Reading 3	Alipay, Singapore Tourism Board provide 1st cashless trip for Chinese tourists 支付宝、新加坡旅游局为中国游客提供第一次无现金旅行

Chapter 6 Education 教育

/71	Reading 1	Economics teachers win awards for using apps to mark scripts and help students keep up with lessons 经济学教师因使用应用程序标记文本帮助学生学业进步而获奖
/74	Reading 2	UKM, RCSEd to promote rural surgery training UKM,RCSEd推进农村地区外科手术培训项目
/77	Reading 3	Top science high schools create innovative energy solutions in competition 顶级中学在竞争中找到创新的能源解决方案

Chapter 7 Culture 文化

/85	Reading 1	Singaporean PM Encourages More Efforts to Use Mandarin 新加坡总理鼓励更多努力使用普通话

目 录

Reading 2　Vietnam's Booming Craft Beer Scene
　　　　　越南蓬勃发展的精酿啤酒业　　　　　　　　　/88

Reading 3　Poor, Rural Students in Laos Lack Tech to Learn
　　　　　From Home
　　　　　老挝贫穷的农村学生缺乏在家里学习的技术设备　/92

Chapter 8　Environment 环境

Reading 1　Bacteria and Fungi Show a Precise Daily Rhythm
　　　　　in Tropical Air
　　　　　热带空气中细菌与真菌呈现精确的每日节奏　　　/99

Reading 2　Better Protection Sought for Thailand's Helmeted
　　　　　Hornbill
　　　　　泰国寻求更好保护盔犀鸟的方法　　　　　　　　/102

Reading 3　Indonesia Province Shuts Schools as Haze from
　　　　　Fires Returns
　　　　　印尼行政区因大火烟雾致学校停课　　　　　　　/106

Chapter 9　Tourism 旅游

Reading 1　Thai Tourism Targets 10 Percent Growth for
　　　　　60th Anniversary
　　　　　泰国旅游业将在60周年之际实现10%的增长目标　/111

Reading 2　Cambodia Unveils Masterplan to Boost Tourism in
　　　　　2 World Heritage Sites
　　　　　柬埔寨公布振兴两处世界遗产旅游的总体规划　　/114

Reading 3　Record-Breaking, 3740-feet-long Waterslide Opens
　　　　　in Malaysia
　　　　　马来西亚的水上滑道开业　　　　　　　　　　　/117

Keys 参考答案　　　/121
Appendix Ⅰ 附录Ⅰ　/137
Appendix Ⅱ 附录Ⅱ　/143
References 参考文献　/155

Chapter 1 Overview

概況

ASEAN

Reading 1

An Overview of ASEAN
东盟概况

June 3rd, 2019 (World Atlas)

What's ASEAN?

A　The Association of Southeast Asian Nations, more commonly known as ASEAN, was formed on 8 August 1967 in Bangkok, Thailand with the signing of the Declaration (Bangkok Declaration) by the Founding Fathers of ASEAN, namely Indonesia, Malaysia, Philippines, Singapore and Thailand.

B　ASEAN is a regional organization that promotes economic integration and intergovernmental cooperation. It has 10 members, comprising Indonesia, Malaysia, Philippines, Singapore ,Thailand, Brunei Darussalam, Viet Nam, Lao PDR, Myanmar and Cambodia, with a total area of 4.49 million square kilometers and a population of 649 million (up to 2018). The ASEAN Secretariat was set up in February 1976 by the Foreign Ministers of ASEAN, with headquarter located in Jakarta, Indonesia.

The Aim and Purpose of ASEAN

C　The motto of ASEAN is "One Vision, One Identity, One Community". As in the ASEAN Declaration, the tenets and objectives of ASEAN are to accelerate economic growth, social cohesion, and cultural development in the region. Apart from economic and political growth, the organization also promotes political stability in individual countries and encourages collaboration on matters of mutual concern. Also, ASEAN focuses on utilization of better agricultural and industrial processes for the well-being of its citizens. Finally, the organization maintains and promotes co-operation with international organizations that have similar aims and purposes.

The Present Economic Status of the ASEAN Countries

D　ASEAN established a free trade area on January 28, 1992, which promotes the free flow of goods within member states. The organization also created a single market and production base which gave it a competitive advantage in the world market and promoted equitable regional development and integrated its member states to the global economy. Countries like Thailand, Singapore, Philippines, Malaysia, Indonesia, and Brunei have eliminated intra-ASEAN import duties on 99.65% tariffs, and the rest countries have reduced taxes by 98.86% as of 2010. In 2017, its gross domestic product was $7.9 trillion, which makes it the fifth-largest organization in the world.

The Promotion of Culture, Sport, and Tourism

E　ASEAN hosts cultural events like sports and education activities such as the ASEAN Center for Biodiversity to promote regional integration. There are also ASEAN Heritage Parks like the Kinabalu National Park that protect natural resources of the Region. As for tourism, the institutionalization of visa-free travel in the ASEAN region has promoted intra-ASEAN travel. As of 2012, tourism accounted for an estimated 4.6%

of ASEAN GDP directly. It employed about 9.3 million people and provided 25 million jobs linked to tourism.

(402 words)

▶▶▶ Notes

  1. ASEAN(全称为 The Association of Southeast Asian Nations)：东南亚国家联盟，简称为东盟。东盟是东南亚地区以经济合作为基础的政治、经济、安全一体化合作组织，其成员国共有10个：印度尼西亚、马来西亚、菲律宾、新加坡、泰国、达鲁萨兰国（简称文莱）、越南、老挝、缅甸、柬埔寨。

  2. The ASEAN Declaration (Bangkok Declaration)：印度尼西亚、马来西亚、菲律宾、新加坡和泰国在1967年签订的《曼谷宣言》，正式宣告东南亚国家联盟的成立。

  3. The ASEAN Secretariat：东盟秘书处。其总部设在印度尼西亚雅加达(Jakarta)，是服务于东南亚10个成员国的行政机构，监督由这一区域组织启动的计划和制定的纲领，成立于1976年。

  4. Gross Domestic Product(缩写为 GDP)：国内生产总值，是一定时期内、一个国家内的经济活动中所生产出的最终成果的市场总价值。

▶▶▶ Words

  1. promote vt. 促进，提升；推销；发扬
  2. integration n. 整合；合并；混合
  3. comprise vt. 由……组成；由……构成；包含
  4. motto n. 座右铭；格言；警句
  5. accelerate vt. 使……加快，使……增速
       vi. 加速；促进；增加
  6. collaboration n. 合作；勾结；通敌
  7. mutual adj. 共同的；相互的；彼此的
  8. utilization n. 利用；使用
  9. establish vt. 设立；建立；制定；确立；证实
       vi. （植物）定植
  10. eliminate vt. 消除，根除，排除
  11. tariff n. 关税；关税表；价目表；收费表
      vt. 按税率定……的价格
  12. institutionalization n. 制度化；体制化

▶▶▶ Useful Expressions

  1. a single market 单一市场
  2. production base 生产基地
  3. a competitive advantage 竞争优势
  4. free trade area 自由贸易区
  5. competitive advantage 竞争优势

Chapter 1 Overview 概况

Difficult Sentences

1. It has 10 members comprising Indonesia, Malaysia, Philippines, Singapore, Thailand, Brunei Darussalam, Viet Nam, Lao PDR, Myanmar and Cambodia, with a total area of 4.49 million square kilometers and a population of 649 million (up to 2018).

本句的主干结构是 It has 10 members，现在分词 comprising 引导的句子充当后置定语，相当于 which comprises...；with a total area of... 在句中充当伴随性状语。

译文：它有 10 个成员国，包括印度尼西亚、马来西亚、菲律宾、新加坡、泰国、文莱、越南、老挝、缅甸和柬埔寨，总面积 449 万平方公里，人口 6.49 亿（截至 2018 年）。

2. The organization also created a single market and production base which gave it a competitive advantage in the world market and promoted equitable regional development and integrated its member states to the global economy.

本句中 which 引导的定语从句修饰 a single market and production base。

译文：东盟也成立了单一市场和生产基地，使它能够在世界市场上获得竞争优势，促进公平的区域发展，使其成员国的经济融合到世界经济之中。

Reading Comprehension

There are five statements attached to the passage containing information given in one of the paragraphs. Identify the paragraph from which the information is derived and each paragraph is marked with a letter. You may only choose one paragraph once. Write down the letter in the blanks of each statement.

_____ 1. ASEAN promotes regional integration by organizing cultural activities.

_____ 2. 10 member states of ASEAN cover the area of 4.49 million square kilometers and a population of approximately 649 million.

_____ 3. The aim and purpose of ASEAN are to promote economic growth, social cohesion, and cultural development in the region.

_____ 4. Founded on 8 August 1967, ASEAN stands for The Association of Southeast Asian Nations.

_____ 5. ASEAN's GDP ranks fifth in the world in 2017.

Reading and Discussion

1. What else does ASEAN boost except for economic and political growth?
2. How does ASEAN promote the free flow of goods within member states?
3. What does ASEAN do to promote the tourism within ASEAN state members?

Language in Use

Complete each sentence with a word listed below. Make changes where necessary.

promote establish mutual accelerate comprise

1. The UN has _____ detailed criteria for who should be allowed to vote.

2. You don't have to sacrifice environmental protection to _____ economic growth.

3. The East and the West can work together for their _____ benefit and progress.

4. Growth will _____ to 2.9 percent next year.

5. Twelve departments _____ this university.

Reading 2

ASEAN Pledges to Ensure Food Security during COVID-19 Outbreak
东盟承诺在 COVID-19 疫情期间确保粮食安全

April 17th, 2020 (https://asean.org)

A Deeply concerned with the potential impact of the COVID-19 outbreak on ASEAN cooperation in food, agriculture and forestry and the disruption of the food supply chain in the region, the ASEAN Ministers on Agriculture and Forestry (AMAF) issued a Joint Statement on 15 April reaffirming commitment to ensure food security, food safety and nutrition in the region during this outbreak.

B The current AMAF Chair Dato Ali Apong, Minister of Primary Resources and Tourism of Brunei Darussalam, expressed his appreciation to his AMAF counterparts for their cooperation and collaboration. He affirmed that ASEAN will continue working to ensure the sustainable supply of sufficient, safe and nutritious food that meet the dietary requirement of ASEAN populations during and after the outbreak of the COVID-19.

C While it is too early to assess the full impact of COVID-19, the pandemic-related disruptions on travel and supply chain markets will have potential risks on the availability and prices of food and agriculture produce in the region depending on the duration of the outbreak and the severity of containment measures needed. There will be immediate effects resulting from such measures adopted by several countries, and these measures will also have long-term effects on agriculture and livelihood, including the ASEAN economy on a broader scale.

D The AMAF pledged, among others, to minimize disruptions in regional food supply chains by working closely together to ensure that markets are kept open and transportation of agricultural and food products are facilitated. They also stressed the importance of reducing excessive price volatility particularly price spikes, ensuring adequate emergency food and reserves and providing timely and accurate market information.

E The ministers urged the ASEAN Member States (AMS) to implement necessary measures, projects and programmes at the national level to meet the immediate food needs of the ASEAN population, particularly the vulnerable groups in the society. Further, they highlighted the need to boost AMS' social protection programmes for smallholder farmers, and Micro, Small and Medium Enterprises to increase food production and ensure food security in the region.

F Mitigating the impact of COVID-19 essentially needs assessment study to determine the effectiveness of mitigation measures on food security and livelihood. The AMS are discussing a study focusing on the challenges and solutions undertaken by each ASEAN Member State to reduce disruptions in food and agriculture trade before, during and after the COVID-19 outbreak. The study will provide recommendations and advice to all AMS on how to address these challenges effectively.

(409 words)

Notes

1. COVID-19：指新型冠状病毒病。其中，"CO"代表Corona（冠状），"VI"代表Virus（病毒），"D"代表Disease（疾病），"19"代表疾病发现的年份2019年。

2. ASEAN Ministers on Agriculture and Forestry (AMAF)：东盟农业和林业部长会议，其目的是充分利用农业和工业扩大贸易、改善交通运输,在提高东盟人民生活水平方面进行更有效的合作。

Words

1. outbreak   n.（战争的）爆发,（疾病的）发作；暴乱
2. disruption n. 扰乱,中断；瓦解
3. commitment n. 承诺,保证；承担义务
4. ensure   vt. 保证,确保；使安全
5. counterpart n.（契约文本等的）副本；互为补充的人或物；极相似的人或物
6. affirm   vt. 肯定；断言
            vi.（不经宣誓而）确认；断言
7. sustainable adj. 可以忍受的；可持续的
8. assess   vt. 评定；估价；对……征税
9. pledge   n. 保证,誓言；抵押；抵押品,典当物
           vt. 保证,许诺；用……抵押；举杯祝……健康
           vi. 许诺；祝酒
10. implement   vt. 实施,执行；实现,使生效
              n. 工具,器具；手段
11. vulnerable   adj. 易受攻击的；易受伤害的；脆弱的
12. mitigate   vt. 使缓和；减轻
            vi. 减轻,缓和下来

Useful Expressions

1. cooperation and collaboration 合作与协作
2. increase food production 提高食品产量
3. ensure food security 确保食品安全

Difficult Sentences

1. While it is too early to assess the full impact of COVID-19, the pandemic-related disruptions on travel and supply chain markets will have potential risks on the availability and prices of food and agriculture produce in the region depending on the duration of the outbreak and the severity of containment measures needed.

本句中,while 引导让步状语从句,and 引导的形容词短语 the pandemic-related disruptions 和名词短语 supply chain markets 充当主句的主语,depending 引导分词短语表伴随的状态。

译文:虽然现在评估 COVID-19 的全面影响还为时过早,但受疫情影响的旅游业和供应链市场将对该地区食品和农产品的供应和价格构成潜在风险,这取决于疫情的持续时间和需要采取的控制措施的严重程度。

2. The AMAF pledged, among others, to minimise disruptions in regional food supply chains by working closely together to ensure that markets are kept open and transportation of agricultural and food products are facilitated.

本句中,主句是 THE AMAF pledged to minimise disruptions in regional food supply chains。among others 是插入语,by working closely together to ensure 是方式状语,that 引导宾语从句充当 ensure 的宾语。

译文:东盟农业和林业部长们承诺,通过他们的密切合作,确保市场保持开放,促进农产品和食品运输,最大限度地减少(疫情)对区域食品供应链的干扰。

Reading Comprehension

There are five statements attached to the passage containing information given in one of the paragraphs. Identify the paragraph from which the information is derived and each paragraph is marked with a letter. You may only choose one paragraph once. Write down the letter in the blanks of each statement.

_____ 1. Mitigation of the influences of COVID-19 will primarily require evaluation studies to decide whether the mitigation measures on food security and livelihood is effective or not.

_____ 2. The measures taken by some countries will have an immediate effect, especially a long-term impact on agriculture and people's livelihoods.

_____ 3. A Joint Statement was signed by AMAF in April.

_____ 4. To meet the food needs of vulnerable groups, the necessary methods will be carried out at the national level.

_____ 5. The present Chair of AMAF was indebted to his AMAF counterparts for their cooperation and collaboration.

Reading and Discussion

1. What did the current AMAF Chair confirm?
2. What's the promise made by the AMAF?
3. What will the study provide for all AMS?

Language in Use

Complete each sentence with a word listed below. Make changes where necessary.

outbreak   pledge   sustainable   implement   mitigate

1. The government promised to _____ a new system to control financial loan institutions.

2. The COVID-19 _____ has been contained.

3. Do our successes _____ our failures?

4. Management has given a _____ that there will be no job losses this year.

5. Try to buy wood that you know has come from a _____ source.

Reading 3

ASEAN Holds Dialogue on the Rights of Persons with Disabilities
东盟举行讨论残疾人权利对话

December 5th, 2018 (https://asean.org)

A The ASEAN Intergovernmental Commission on Human Rights (AICHR) convened the 2018 Dialogue to mainstream the rights of persons with disabilities in the ASEAN Community from 3 to 5 December in Bangkok.

B It was the fourth annual dialogue conducted with a view to fostering the realization of the rights of persons with disabilities in all community pillars of ASEAN.

C Focusing on the theme "Accessibility Through Universal Design", the dialogue gathered participants from ASEAN sectoral bodies, government officials, organizations of persons with disabilities, national human rights institutions and experts on disability rights. Participants exchanged views and shared experiences in the application of universal design as key to achieve accessibility in various spheres beyond physical environment, including in financial services, access to justice and access to information.

D The dialogue commenced with the launch of the "ASEAN Enabling Masterplan 2025: Mainstreaming the Rights of Persons with Disabilities" in conjunction with commemoration of the International Day of Persons with Disabilities.

E In his opening remarks, delivered through a video, Thailand's Prime Minister Prayuth Chan-o-cha welcomed the launching of the ASEAN Enabling Masterplan which aims to make the region an accessible and inclusive community for all.

General Anantaporn Kanjanarat, Minister of Social Development and Human Security of Thailand, in his remarks underlined that access to information and technology was key for empowerment of persons with disabilities. The launch of the ASEAN Enabling Masterplan was also welcomed by the Executive Secretary of the UNESCAP Armida Salsiah Alisjahbana, Deputy Secretary-General of ASEAN for ASEAN Political-Security Community Hoang Anh Tuan and the Ambassador of Japan to ASEAN Kazuo

Sunaga.

F During the three-day dialogue, participants and resource persons highlighted universal design as precondition to enabling environment and the need for public-private-people partnership with participation of persons with disabilities and organisations of persons with disabilities to ensure accessibility and inclusion. Empowering persons with disabilities to understand and exercise their rights and the use of information and communication technology to enhance accessibility were also highlighted.

G The dialogue was organized by Dr. Seree Nonthasoot, the Representative of Thailand to the AICHR with support from Japan-ASEAN Integration Fund and the Australian Government.

(347 words)

Notes

1. The ASEAN Intergovernmental Commission on Human Rights (AICHR)：东盟政府间人权委员会，主要任务是促进和保护东盟国家在人权方面的交流与合作。

2. ASEAN Community：东盟共同体，即东南亚国家联盟作为一个整体出现。

3. Ministry of Social Development and Human Security of Thailand：泰国国家社会发展与人类安全部，主要职责为保护弱势群体权益。

4. The International Day of Persons with Disabilities：国际残疾人日。每年的 12 月 3 日是"国际残疾人日"，旨在促进人们对残疾问题的理解和动员人们维护残疾人的尊严、权利和幸福。

Words

1. convene   vt. 召集，集合；传唤……出庭受审
             vi. 聚集，集合
2. mainstream n. 主流
              adj. 主流的
              v. 把(残疾人)转入正规班级(或工作岗位)
3. disability n. 残疾；无能力；(律)无资格；不利条件
4. foster   v. 促进；养育
            adj. 收养的；收养孤儿的
5. participant   n. 参与者，参加者
                adj. 参与的
6. commence   vt. 着手；使开始
             vi. 开始
7. inclusive adj. 包含的，包括的
8. underline vt. 强调；在……下面划线；预告
             n. 下划线；(戏单下面的)下期节目预告
9. highlight vt. 使突出，强调，使显著；照亮
             n. 最精彩的部分，最重要的事情；强光(效果)

Chapter 1　Overview 概况

Useful Expressions

1. universal design 通用设计
2. opening remarks 开幕词
3. financial services 金融服务
4. the use of information and communication technology 信息和通信技术的使用

Difficult Sentences

1. Participants exchanged views and shared experiences in the application of universal design as key to achieve accessibility in various spheres beyond physical environment, including in financial services, access to justice and access to information.

本句中 to achieve.... environment 为动词不定式短语做目的性状语, including... information 是介词短语做状语。

译文：与会者就通用化设计的应用交换了意见和分享了经验, 认为通用化设计是在物理环境以外的各种领域实现无障碍的关键, 包括金融服务、诉讼司法和信息的获取。

2. During the three-day dialogue, participants and resource persons highlighted universal design as precondition to enabling environment and the need for public-private-people partnership with participation of persons with disabilities and organizations of persons with disabilities to ensure accessibility and inclusion.

本句中, during 引导时间状语从句, "在……期间"; 第一个 to 为介词, 引导的介词短语做定语修饰 precondition; 第二个 to ensure accessibility and inclusion 是动词不定式做目的性状语。

译文：在为期三天的对话中, 与会者和资源管理人员强调：通用化设计是确保残疾人可以参与政府企业公民跨界合作和有残疾人参与机构活动的环境和需求的可行性和包容性的先决条件。

Reading Comprehension

There are five statements attached to the passage containing information given in one of the paragraphs. Identify the paragraph from which the information is derived and each paragraph is marked with a letter. You may only choose one paragraph once. Write down the letter in the blanks of each statement.

_____ 1. The dialogue began with the opening of ASEAN Enabling Masterplan 2025.

_____ 2. With the goal of facilitating the rights of persons with disabilities, the dialogue is convened yearly.

_____ 3. Opinions and experience about the application of universal design were discussed by attendees during the dialogue.

_____ 4. Importance was also attached to strengthen accessibility by using information and communication technology.

_____ 5. The 2018 Dialogue on the rights of persons with disabilities was held in Bangkok.

▶▶▶ Reading and Discussion

1. What's purpose of the 2018 Dialogue held by AICHR?

2. What's the participants' point of view towards the application of universal design?

3. How long did the meeting last?

▶▶▶ Language in Use

Complete each sentence with a word listed below. Make changes where necessary.

foster   underline   highlight   commence   participant

1. This incident _____ the danger of travelling in the border area.

2. Of course we must _____ that the system can hardly be inaccurate.

3. If you have time, please answer a comment of another _____.

4. He said that developed countries had a responsibility to _____ global economic growth to help new democracies.

5. They _____ a systematic search.

Chapter 2 Current Politics

时政

ASEAN

前言

Reading 1

Indonesia will build its new capital city in Borneo as Jakarta sinks into the Java Sea
印尼总统决定迁都

Aug 26th, 2019(CNN)

A A jungle-draped area on the east of Borneo island is set to be transformed into Indonesia's new capital city, President Joko Widodo announced Monday, amid concerns over the sustainability of its congested and rapidly sinking political center Jakarta.

B The proposed location, near the relatively underdeveloped cities of Balikpapan and Samarinda, is a far cry from the crowded powerhouse which has served as Indonesia's financial heart since 1949 — and Widodo acknowledged that moving the country's capital to the island will be a mammoth and expensive undertaking. But Jakarta's rapid expansion in recent years has presented myriad environmental, economic and safety concerns, prompting the government to look elsewhere and ease the strain on the massive metropolis.

C "As a large nation that has been independent for 74 years, Indonesia has never chosen its own capital," Widodo said in a televised speech, AFP reported, "The burden Jakarta is holding right now is too heavy as the center of governance, business, finance, trade and services."

D The ambitious project to move the capital will likely cost around 486 trillion rupiah ($34 billion), CNN Indonesia reported, and officials have previously said the relocation could take around 10 years.

E Jakarta is home to more than 10 million people, according to the United Nations, with an estimated 30 million in the greater metropolitan area — making it one of the world's most overpopulated urban regions.

F It's also one of the fastest-sinking cities on Earth, according to the World Economic Forum, dropping into the Java Sea at an alarming rate due to over-extraction of groundwater. The city sits on swampy ground and hugs the sea to the north, making it especially prone to flooding.

G A worsening air pollution crisis, exacerbated by near-constant traffic congestion on its roads, has grown so dire that some residents sued the Indonesian government in July.

H No name has been given for the new site, but the government originally announced plans to relocate the capital in April. The move requires parliamentary approval to be given the go-ahead.

I Indonesia owns the majority of Borneo, the world's third-largest island, with Malaysia and Brunei each holding parts of its northern region. The island is covered in vast rainforests, but it has been hit by rampant deforestation in recent years.

(401 words)

Notes

1. Borneo:婆罗洲,也叫加里曼丹岛,世界第三大岛,面积 74.33 万平方千米,属于热带雨林气候,植被繁茂。

2. Jakarta:雅加达,印尼首都及最大城市。

3. Java Sea:爪哇海,是太平洋西部海域,位于爪哇岛、苏拉威西岛、加里曼丹岛、苏门答腊岛之间,东北连望加锡海峡,东邻弗洛勒斯海,西南接巽他海峡(通印度洋),西北为邦加岛和勿里洞岛。东西长约 1450 千米,南北长约 420 千米,总面积约为 43.3 万平方千米。

4. Balikpapan:巴厘巴板,是位于加里曼丹岛的印度尼西亚城市,位于东加里曼丹省东南部。巴厘巴板是加里曼丹岛的金融中心和最大的经济体,也是东加里曼丹省最大的城市,一直是印度尼西亚最宜居的城市之一。

5. Samarinda:三马林达市,是印度尼西亚东加里曼丹省首府,位于加里曼丹岛东部,望加锡海峡西岸。主要农作物有大米、蔬菜、木薯和红薯。

6. rupiah:印度尼西亚卢比,是印度尼西亚的法定货币。

7. World Economic Forum:世界经济论坛,因在瑞士达沃斯首次举办,又被称为"达沃斯论坛"。是以研究和探讨世界经济领域存在的问题、促进国际经济合作与交流为宗旨的非官方国际性机构,总部设在瑞士日内瓦。

Words and Expressions

1. transform   n. 转换句
             vt. 使改观,使改变性质(或结构等),使改变性情(或个性);改造
             vi. 变形;转换
2. sustainability   n. 耐久性;可持续发展
3. congest   vt.(常用于被动语态)堵塞,拥挤,挤满;使充血
           vi. 拥挤;充血
4. powerhouse   n. 强国,权势集团;发电厂;(口)身强体壮的人,精力充沛的人
5. mammoth   n. 猛犸(象);庞然大物
           adj. 巨大的,庞大的
6. undertaking   n. 任务,企业,事业;保证;承担
7. myriad   n. 无数;大量
          adj. 无数的;各式各样的
8. governance   n. 统治;管理;管理体系;统治权
9. ambitious   adj. 有抱负的,志向远大的,雄心勃勃的;要求过高的
10. extraction   n. 提取,提炼,拔出,开采;血统;拔出物;拔出术
11. groundwater   n. 地下水
12. swampy   adj.(指地面)湿软的,沼泽地的
13. prone   adj. 易于……的,有……倾向的;卧倒的
14. exacerbate   vt. 使恶化,使加重,使加剧

15. dire   adj. 严重的,危急的,极端的
16. sue   vt. 控告,对……提起诉讼
         vi. 控告,起诉
17. parliamentary   adj. 议会的
18. go-ahead   n. (有关当局)认可,许可;进取心
             adj. 前进的
19. rampant   adj. 猖獗的,泛滥的
20. deforestation   n. 大面积砍伐森林;人为毁林

Useful Expressions

1. jungle-draped area 丛林覆盖区域
2. a far cry from 与……有很大差别
3. at an alarming rate 以惊人的速度
4. swampy ground 沼泽地,低湿地

Difficult Sentences

1. The proposed location, near the relatively underdeveloped cities of Balikpapan and Samarinda, is a far cry from the crowded powerhouse which has served as Indonesia's financial heart since 1949 — and Widodo acknowledged that moving the country's capital to the island will be a mammoth and expensive undertaking.

本句中 which 从句修饰 powerhouse,表示 powerhouse 从 1949 年以来一直是印尼金融中心,因此可以推断出此处的 powerhouse 指代的是首都雅加达。

译文:新首都位于相对不发达的巴厘巴板和沙马林达附近,与 1949 年以来一直是印尼金融中心的拥挤的大都市雅加达相去甚远。维多多承认,迁都至该岛将是一项庞大而昂贵的工程。

2. But Jakarta's rapid expansion in recent years has presented myriad environmental, economic and safety concerns, prompting the government to look elsewhere and ease the strain on the massive metropolis.

本句的谓语 has presented 后的宾语是由 myriad environmental, economic and safety 修饰的 concerns,现在分词 promoting 作状语。

译文:但近年来雅加达的快速扩张引发了环境、经济和安全等种种问题,促使政府将目光投向别处,以缓解这座大都市的压力。

3. A worsening air pollution crisis, exacerbated by near-constant traffic congestion on its roads, has grown so dire that some residents sued the Indonesian government in July.

本句中 so...that... 表示"如此……以至于……",that 引导结果状语从句。

译文:常年的交通堵塞使不断恶化的空气污染危机变得非常可怕,一些居民在 7 月份起诉了印尼政府。

Reading Comprehension

There are five statements attached to the passage containing information given in one of the paragraphs. Identify the paragraph from which the information is derived and each paragraph is marked with a letter. You may only choose one paragraph once. Write down the letter in the blanks of each statement.

_____ 1. The government has not named its new capital, but in April it announced the plan of moving the capital which need to be voted through by the parliament to be carried out.

_____ 2. According to the UN, with over 10 million people reside in Jakarta and approximately 30 million in the greater metropolitan area, it is the most densely populated urban regions.

_____ 3. Jakarta is sinking very fast according to the date of World Economic Forum because the groundwater were over extracted, and it is sinking at a dramatical speed into the Java Sea.

_____ 4. Worrying about sustainable development of Jakarta, the overcrowded political center of Indonesia, the relocation of capital was announced Monday by President Joko Widodo.

_____ 5. The government has to seek solution to cope with stress on Jakarta due to innumerable worries on environment, economy and safety.

Reading and Discussion

1. Which city does the word "powerhouse" refer to?
2. Why is Jakarta sinking?
3. Why was the Indonesian government sued by some residents?

Language in Use

Complete each sentence with a word listed below. Make changes where necessary.

governance   exacerbate   myriad   congest   dire

1. The programmes may not be to blame. The problem may lie with the _____ quality of schools and clinics.

2. WHO is helping to manage these at the _____ airports, to ensure that the right medicines and equipment are distributed to the right places.

3. Analysts said the BRIC proposals were premature and could _____ the global crisis.

4. It has been a critical task for banking industry to continuously improve its corporate _____ to meet the request of market development.

5. As part of the build-up to Copenhagen, the United Nations is hosting a series of major meetings to try to reach agreement on _____ issues.

Chapter 2　Current Politics　时政

Reading 2

Gov't looking to strengthen laws on data protection
修正法案促网络安全

October 31th, 2019(BERNAMA)

A　The government is in the midst of improving existing laws on data protection to counter the challenges and cyber threats faced today.

B　Referring to a recent hacking incident involving the University of Malaya's (UM) e-pay portal on Thursday, Communications and Multimedia Minister Gobind Singh Deo said the improvements were also in line with the development of new technologies as part of efforts to maintain data security.

C　"In our country, we have laws that have been in place since 2010, and I think we have reached a point where we need to improve on it.

D　"To me, the current law is enforceable, but at the same time we need to look at how we can implement amendments to strengthen and tighten existing laws to meet the challenges and threats we face today," he said.

E　Gobind said this while winding up his debate on the Supply Bill 2020 on behalf of his ministry at the Dewan Rakyat yesterday.

F　He said the Amendment Bill was expected to be tabled during the next Parliament session between March and May 2020.

G　"I am in the process of improving the existing provision to address cyber security and data security issues," he said. Meanwhile, on efforts to accelerate the digital economy, Gobind said a partnership with the Malaysia Digital Economy Corporation (MDEC) through the eUsahawan programme and the Go-eCommerce platform have benefited 306,849 entrepreneurs.

H　"We provide training opportunities and content for micro and youth entrepreneurs to gain knowledge in digital entrepreneurship including marketing through social media, e-marketplaces, data analysis, online payments, digital advertising and cyber security," he said.

I　Gobind also noted that out of the total, 107,558 entrepreneurs managed to generate additional sales online totalling RM586 million.

J　Referring to the proposal to set up the Digital Economy Special Council, Gobind welcomed the proposal, but said the ministry was currently focusing on the Malaysia Multimedia Super Corridor Implementation Council Meeting to discuss topics related to the digital economy.

(356 words)

 Notes

1. Gobind Singh Deo：哥宾星，马来西亚通信与多媒体部长。

2. Dewan Rakyat：马来西亚下议院。1957 年马来西亚独立后，仿效英国模式建立了两院制议会，包括上议院（Senate，马来文为 Dewan Negara）和下议院（House of Representatives，马来文为 Dewan Rakyat）。上议院共 70 席，其中 26 名是由全国 13 个州议会各选举产生 2 名，其余 44 名由最高元首根据内阁推荐委任，任期 3 年，可连任两届。下议院共设议席 222 个，任期 5 年，可连任。

3. Malaysia Multimedia Super Corridor Implementation Council Meeting：马来西亚多媒体超级走廊实施委员会会议，多媒体超级走廊（Multimedia Super Corridor，简称 MSC）是马来西亚政府促进国家科技发展的计划。多媒体超级走廊覆盖面积为 15 千米宽，50 千米长，坐落于吉隆坡市中心。

4. Malaysia Digital Economy Corporation：马来西亚数字经济发展局，成立于 1996 年，致力于管理及领导马来西亚的数字经济发展。

Words

1. Gov't ＝ government 政府
2. hack　vt. 砍，切，劈；未经允许侵入他人的计算机系统（来窃取信息或从事非法勾当）
　　　　vi. 砍，劈；短促频繁地干咳；非法闯入电脑网络
　　　　n. 砍；砍痕；企图
3. portal　n. 门户站点；门，入口
4. enforceable　adj. 可实施的；可强制执行的
5. implement　vt. 实施，贯彻；补充；向……提供工具（或手段）
　　　　n. 工具；装备
6. amendment　n. 修改，修订；修正案，修正条款
7. session　n.（议会等机构）会议；（法庭的）开庭
8. provision　n. 提供；供给；规定，条款
　　　　vt. 向……供应食物和其他必需品
　　　　vi.（公司等）留出资金以备
9. accelerate　vt. 使加快，使增速；促进，促使……早日发生
　　　　vi. 加快；增加
10. entrepreneur　n. 企业家，创业者
11. micro＝microcomputer

Useful Expressions

1. referring to 提到，谈及，谈起
2. in line with 行动符合；符合；和……一致
3. in place 在应有的位置上，已经到位
4. wind up 陷入，卷入，落得

Difficult Sentences

1. To me, the current law is enforceable, but at the same time we need to look at

how we can implement amendments to strengthen and tighten existing laws to meet the challenges and threats we face today.

本句中 implement 是动词,是实施的意思。

译文:我认为,目前的法律是可行的,但是与此同时我们需要思考如何实施修正案才能加强现有的法律,以应对我们今天面临的挑战和威胁。

2. He said the Amendment Bill was expected to be tabled during the next Parliament session between March and May 2020.

本句中 table 用作动词,是把(议案)提交讨论的意思。

译文:他说该修正法案有望在2020年3月至5月间召开的下一届议会会议上提交讨论。

3. Meanwhile, on efforts to accelerate the digital economy, Gobind said a partnership with the Malaysia Digital Economy Corporation (MDEC) through the eUsahawan programme and the Go-eCommerce platform have benefited 306,849 entrepreneurs.

本句中 eUsahawan programme 是马来西亚旨在帮助年轻人成为企业家的项目,Go-eCommerce platform 是马来西亚的一个在线创业平台。

译文:与此同时,哥宾星说在努力加速电子经济增长的同时,马来西亚数字经济发展局与 eUsahawan 项目以及 Go-eCommerce 平台合作,使306849名企业家受益。

》》》Reading Comprehension

There are five statements attached to the passage containing information given in one of the paragraphs. Identify the paragraph from which the information is derived and each paragraph is marked with a letter. You may only choose one paragraph once. Write down the letter in the blanks of each statement.

_____ 1. Gobind said as to making endeavor to boost the digital economy, 306849 company owners have reaped the benefits through the eUsahawan programme by forming a partnership with MDEC.

_____ 2. Training opportunities and contents, including social media, e-marketplaces, data analysis, online payment, digital advertising and online security, are offered to micro and young company owners so that they can learn how to startup their career in digital way.

_____ 3. As far as I am concerned, the law is still in effect, but in order to confront the challenges and threats we need to find solutions by implementing amendments to reinforce and tighten the laws that already exist.

_____ 4. He said he expected the Amendment Bill to be put forward to the Parliament on next session between March and May 2020.

_____ 5. When mentioning that the University of Malaya's e-pay portal suffered attacks from hackers, Gobind, the Communications and Multimedia Minister, said as part of the endeavor to sustain data safety the advances of new technologies should be in accordance with their improvements.

Reading and Discussion

1. What happened to University of Malaya recently?
2. What does Gobind think of the current law concerning cyber and data security?
3. What do the eUsahawan programme and the Go-eCommerce platform provide to entrepreneurs?

Language in Use

Complete each sentence with a word listed below. Make changes where necessary.

implement   accelerate   provision   refer   enforceable

1. On page two of your handout you will find a list of the books that I have _____ to during the lecture.

2. The changes to the national health system will be _____ next year.

3. There are clear, _____ rules regarding intellectual property and copyright protection.

4. Inflation is likely to _____ this year, adding further upward pressure on interest rates.

5. She accepted the job with the _____ that she would be paid expenses for relocating.

Reading 3

Philippines passes law requiring students to plant 10 trees before graduating
菲律宾新法案：想毕业，先种树

June 5th, 2019 (*China Daily*)

A Environmental issues are at the forefront of many people's minds, but it's the younger generation who is particularly concerned about the future of our planet. From global school strikes for climate change action to amazing teen activists, kids are now having to take it into their own hands to ensure they will grow up in a sustainable world. In an effort to foster this love and care for the earth, a new bill has been passed in the Philippines that requires students to plant 10 trees each before graduating.

B The Graduation Legacy for the Environment Act was introduced by congressman Gary Alejano in 2016 in a bid to promote "inter-generational responsibility" for the environment. On May 15, 2019 it was officially passed, marking a huge step in the right direction towards a healthy planet.

C "While we recognize the right of the youth to a balanced and healthy ecology... there is no reason why they cannot be made to contribute in order to ensure that this will be an actual reality," Gary Alejano commented on the bill.

D The Philippines has lost more than 30% of its forest cover due to illegal logging, but the new bill means that the younger generation can help to reverse the issue. Under the new initiative, 175 million new trees could be planted by students each year. If only 10% of them survive, that means that 525 billion trees could flourish over the course of one generation.

E According to the details outlined in the bill, the rule applies to all students in order to graduate primary school, high school, and college. Trees can be planted in either forests, mangroves, reserves, urban areas, abandoned mining sites, or in indigenous territory.

F In fact, this isn't the only positive initiative that involves the younger generation. One school in India made its students pay their "school fees" by collecting, bringing to school, and recycling plastic waste that was lying across the town. This type of initiative helped raise awareness about plastic waste in Asian countries. It also allowed more students to seek education and even helped the students to earn some money by recycling the plastic so they wouldn't have to resort to child labor in order to survive.

(400 words)

Notes

1. Philippines：菲律宾，是菲律宾共和国（Republic of the Philippines）的简称，位于西太平洋，是东南亚一个多民族群岛国家，人口约 1 亿 800 万（2020 年 9 月）。

2. Graduation Legacy for the Environment Act：《毕业回馈环境法》，2016 年，国会议员 Gary Alejano 提出了此法案，旨在促进环境的"代际责任"。它于 2019 年 5 月 15 日正式通过，标志着朝着健康地球的正确方向迈出了一大步。

Words

1. forefront n. 最显要的位置，最重要的地位
2. sustainable adj. 可持续的，能长期保持的
3. foster vt. 收养，代养，抚育；鼓励，促进，培养
    adj. 收养的，代养的
4. bill n. 账单；议案，法案；钞票，纸币
    vt. 给……开账单
5. comment n. 评论，意见，评价，批评
    v. 评论；议论；发表意见
6. logging n. （木材）采运作业
7. reverse vt. 使反向，使倒转；彻底改变
    vi. 反向，倒转
    adj. 反向的；反面的
    n. 对立面
8. initiative n. 倡议；首创精神；主动性
    adj. 初步的，创始的

9. course   n. 课程；进程，进展；航道，路线

     vi. 跑

     vt. 迅速穿过；追

10. mangrove   n. 红树（一种热带乔木，生于水边，盘错交织的部分根部露于地上）

11. indigenous   adj. 当地的，本土的，土生土长的；内在的

12. indigenous territory   原住民地区

13. resort   n. 度假胜地；求助

     vi. 凭借，采用

Useful Expressions

1. strike for   为了……而斗争
2. resort to   依靠
3. child labor   童工

Difficult Sentences

1. The Graduation Legacy for the Environment Act was introduced by congressman Gary Alejano in 2016 in a bid to promote "inter-generational responsibility" for the environment.

  此句的主语是 The Graduation Legacy for the Environment Act，谓语用了被动语态，不定式 to promote 表目的。句中的 bid 表示"努力争取"。

  译文：2016 年，国会议员盖瑞·亚历哈诺提出了《毕业回馈环境法》这一法案，旨在提高人们对环境的"代际责任"意识。

2. One school in India made its students pay their "school fees" by collecting, bringing to school, and recycling plastic waste that was lying across the town.

  本句中 make sb. do sth. 指让某人做某事，made its students pay their "school fees" 的意思是让学生交学费。介词 by 后面跟了三个动名词 collecting, bringing 和 recycling 以表示方法手段。waste 由后面的 that 定语从句修饰。

  译文：在印度，有一所学校让学生收集整个镇上的塑料垃圾，并带到学校来支付"学费"并回收利用。

Reading Comprehension

There are five statements attached to the passage containing information given in one of the paragraphs. Identify the paragraph from which the information is derived and each paragraph is marked with a letter. You may only choose one paragraph once. Write down the letter in the blanks of each statement.

_____ 1. The Philippines has passed a new bill according to which students need to plant 10 trees before leaving school. The aim to this act is to cultivate love and concern for the earth.

_____ 2. In 2016 for the purpose of enhancing sense of responsibility for environment, congressman Gary Alejano introduced the Graduation Legacy for the Environment

Act, which was officially adopted on May 15, 2019 and signified extraordinary progress toward a healthy earth.

_____ 3. 30 percent of Philippine forests was damaged by illegal logging, but the new bill signifies that the young people can help to turn the tide against this.

_____ 4. Students in one India school can pay for their tuition by handing plastic wastes that they collect around the town.

_____ 5. We have the consensus that the younger generation are entitled to an ecology that is balanced and healthy, but there is no ground that all these come without a price.

Reading and Discussion

1. How many trees students are required to plant by the Graduation Legacy for the Environment Act?

2. Why did Philippines lost its forest cover and how many percent is the forest cover lost?

3. What is the other initiative that involves the young mentioned in the news?

Language in Use

Complete each sentence with a word listed below. Make changes where necessary.

forefront　foster　reverse　initiative　indigenous

1. The islanders are trying to protect the island's _____ plant and animal life.

2. The loan of a player is often used to _____ young talented players that would otherwise not find opportunities in a team.

3. The new manager hoped to _____ the decline in the company's fortunes.

4. They may look like an ordinary pair of spectacles, but these glasses are at the _____ of a revolution in eyewear.

5. Although she was quite young, she showed a lot of _____ and was promoted to manager after a year.

Chapter 3 Economy

经济

ASEAN

Reading 1

Southeast Asia's Leaders Call for Faster Asian Economic Integration
东南亚领导人敦促加快地区经济整合

February 28, 2009 (VOA)

A Southeast Asian business and government leaders have urged faster regional economic integration to cushion the impact of the global economic downturn. The call comes as leaders of the 10-member Association of Southeast Asian Nations gather in Thailand for their annual summit.

B With exports from Southeast Asia plummeting, the region's business and government leaders are seeking to bolster trade within Asia to compensate for falling demand in the West.

C Trade among the 10 members of the Association of Southeast Asian Nations (ASEAN) has been expanding, but the leaders say there is still room for further growth. It accounts for only a quarter of ASEAN's total trade. ASEAN officials say this trade should increase by 35 to 40 percent in the next six years.

D At an ASEAN business and investment meeting in Bangkok Friday, Thai Prime Minister Abhisit Vejjajiva said this week's Leaders Summit would push harder for the realization of a common market by 2015.

E "Already we have seen tremendous growth in intra-ASEAN trade and investment," Mr. Abhisit said. "But the fact of the matter is, we have not done enough and we have to do much, much more."

F ASEAN has a combined market of more than 500 million people. In recent years, ASEAN has pushed to expand access for its products within Asia by signing free trade agreements with Japan, China and South Korea — a combined market of about two billion people.

G That trading area will further widen to include Australia and New Zealand, which will sign free trade agreements with ASEAN Friday. India is expected to do the same in April.

H Narongchai Akrasanee, chairman of the Export—Import Bank of Thailand and the country's former commerce minister, said the global economic crisis would accelerate Asian economic integration as neighbors turn to each other for investment and trade.

I "We have so much [foreign currency] reserves in our countries, about $4 trillion, and we talk about using these reserves for our investments, to support our projects, in our land," said Narongchai. "Now circumstances would force us to make use of this."

J Earlier this week, ASEAN, China, Japan and South Korea agreed to expand a regional fund aimed at helping Asian governments facing liquidity problems.

K Arin Jira, the chairman of the ASEAN Business Advisory Council, says although times are difficult, some of the region's top businesses see the current crisis as a chance for the region to lead the global recovery.

L "We shall no longer be running around following the other advanced economies," said Arin. "We will lead the world out of this crisis and I think we can do it because we are better cushioned than before."

M ASEAN was formed in 1967 to promote political and economic cooperation. Its annual summit opens Saturday in the Thai resort town of Cha-am, 200 kilometers south of the capital.

(465 words)

Notes

1. Thai Prime Minister Abhisit Vejjajiva：泰国总理阿披实·维乍集瓦。
2. Narongchai Akrasanee, chairman of the Export-Import Bank of Thailand：泰国进出口银行行长纳隆猜·阿卡拉沙尼。
3. Arin Jira, the chairman of the ASEAN Business Advisory Council：东盟工商咨询委员会主席阿兰·伊拉。
4. Thai resort town of Cha-am：泰国度假胜地七岩，位于泰国巴蜀府的华欣七岩，以碧海、沙滩、椰影的南国风光闻名于世，也是泰国皇室贵族最钟爱的避暑胜地，拥有风格独特、优雅动人的度假气氛。

Words

1. integration   n. 结合，整合；整体
2. downturn   n. (商业经济的) 衰退，下降
3. cushion   n. 软垫，坐垫，靠垫；起保护(或缓冲)作用的事物
            v. (跌倒或碰撞时) 起缓冲作用，缓和冲击，使松软
4. gather   vi. 聚集，聚拢，集合；逐渐增加
           vt. 使聚拢，挑选
           n. 收缩；聚集
5. summit   vi. 参加峰会；登上顶峰
           n. 最高点，山顶；(政府间的) 首脑会议；峰会
           adj. 最高级的，政府首脑间的
6. plummet   vi. 暴跌，速降
            n. 铅坠
7. bolster   v. 支承，加固；支持，提高
            n. 垫枕
8. compensate   vt. 偿还，补偿，付报酬
               vi. 赔偿
9. impact   n. 冲击(力)，冲突，影响(力)
           vt. 压紧；充满
           vi. 冲击，碰撞；有不良影响
10. expanding   adj. 扩展的，扩充的

11. accelerate   vt. 使……加快;使……增速
                 vi. 加速
12. current   n. (水、气、电)流;趋势
                 adj. 流通的;当前的
13. recovery   n. 恢复,复原,痊愈

Useful Expressions

1. common market 共同市场
2. free trade agreement 自由贸易协定
3. former commerce minister 前商务部部长
4. liquidity problems 资金流问题

Difficult Sentences

1. With exports from Southeast Asia plummeting, the region's business and government leaders are seeking to bolster trade within Asia to compensate for falling demand in the West.

本句中 with exports...plummeting 是独立主格结构作状语表原因,主句为 the region's business and government leaders are seeking to bolster trade within Asia,其后的不定式短语 to compensate for falling demand in the West 表目的。

译文:由于东南亚的出口量急剧下跌,该地区的工商界和政府领导人寻求推动亚洲内部贸易的方法,以弥补西方需求量下降的差额。

2. "We shall no longer be running around following the other advanced economies," said Arin. "We will lead the world out of this crisis and I think we can do it because we are better cushioned than before."

run around:东奔西跑,cushion:缓冲,缓解。

译文:阿兰说:"我们不必再跟在其他发达经济体的后面瞎跑。我们将引导世界走出这次危机。我认为我们做得到,因为比起以往,我们有了更大的承受能力。"

Reading Comprehension

There are five statements attached to the passage containing information given in one of the paragraphs. Identify the paragraph from which the information is derived and each paragraph is marked with a letter. You may only choose one paragraph once. Write down the letter in the blanks of each statement.

_____ 1. The leaders of 10 countries demand the yearly meeting to hold in Thailand.

_____ 2. According to Thai Prime Minister Abhisit Vejjajiva, the goal of this summit is to make efforts to achieve the trade freely among ASEA members and make common decisions about industry and agriculture by 2015.

_____ 3. ASEAN has developed a commercial treaty with more Asian countries as Japan, China and South Korea.

_____ 4. The economic cooperation among Asian countries goes faster and faster to cope with the worldwide negative financial growth.

_____ 5. Asian countries don't need to just follow the western countries in developing economy but to lead the world to face the economic challenge.

Reading and Discussion

Work in groups to discuss the following questions.

1. Why have Southeast Asian business and government leaders urged faster regional economic integration?

2. What is the main purpose of this week's Leaders Summit?

3. Why does Arin Jira, the chairman of the ASEAN Business Advisory Council, see the current crisis as a chance for the region to lead global recovery?

Language in Use

Complete each sentence with a word listed below. Make changes where necessary.

bolster   downturn   plummet   accelerate   integration

1. There is the evidence of a _____ in the housing market.

2. Several large rocks were sent _____ down the mountain.

3. Inflation is likely to _____ this year, adding further upward pressure on interest rates.

4. The aim of this summit is to promote closer economic _____ among countries.

5. Hopes of an early cut in interest rates would _____ confidence.

Reading 2

Singapore Monetary, Fiscal Policy "Appropriate" for Now: MAS
新加坡金融管理局:现在执行"恰当的"新加坡金融与财政政策

October 30th, 2019(excerpt from *The Business Times*)

A SINGAPORE'S recently loosened monetary policy, and its fiscal policy, taken together, are "appropriate given current economic conditions", the Monetary Authority of Singapore (MAS) reiterated-giving a more short-term opinion than was stated earlier in the year.

B The government's fiscal stance for 2019 is still expected to be "mildly expansionary", according to the MAS half-yearly macroeconomic review, released on Wednesday. But, while the Singapore Budget tends to be mildly stimulatory, the size of the expected boost has eased.

C "This macroeconomic policy mix is assessed to be appropriate given current economic conditions," the central bank said in its latest biannual report, while re-affirming that, "should the outlook for inflation and growth weaken significantly, MAS is prepared to recalibrate monetary policy".

D By stressing ongoing conditions, the MAS tacitly gazes closer into the crystal ball than it did in April, when policies were tipped to ensure "price stability and sustainable growth in the medium term". Singapore's fiscal impulse, which measures how government spending affects the economy in the shortterm, has been pegged at about 0.4 percent of gross domestic product (GDP) for the year.

E That figure still "implies a slightly more expansionary fiscal policy stance" than in 2018, but is lower than the estimate of 0.7 percent in the April macroeconomic review.

F This year's expansionary fiscal impulse - which means that the government has taken out less revenue than it is spending, against the year before - follows initiatives from a "longer - term sustainable growth" Budget that the MAS noted were meant to raise productivity and tackle social inequality.

G Since then, though, the output gap "has turned slightly negative", as the MAS noted in its monetary policy statement earlier in October.

H "While a slowdown in Singapore's trade - related sectors was anticipated, the extent of the downshift in activity in the last six months turned out to be more severe than previously envisaged," the MAS noted in its October macroeconomic review report.

I Despite the turn to expansionary macroeconomic policy in economies elsewhere, the MAS has warned that "constraints such as policy space, debt sustainability and financial stability concerns could cap the stimulus to these economies".

J Still, key differences between Singapore and other economies involve the central bank's use of the Singdollar exchange rate, rather than interest rates, in monetary policy, as well as its fiscal headroom in terms of its low debt constraints, ample reserves, and surpluses from previous national Budgets.

(435 words)

》》》Notes

1. Monetary Authority of Singapore (MAS):新加坡金融管理局。它是新加坡行使中央银行职能的金融机构,归财政部所属。全面行使一般中央银行的职权,包括指导金融业、监督银行的各项经营行为。

2. Singdollar:新加坡元。即 Singapore dollar,是新加坡的法定货币,以 S$ 标记。

》》》Words

1. monetary   adj. 货币的;金融的
2. fiscal   adj. 财政的;国库的
3. reiterate   vt. 重申;反复做
4. macroeconomic   adj. 宏观经济的
5. stimulatory   vt. 刺激;激励;鼓舞
              adj. 起刺激作用的
              vi. 起刺激作用

6. biannual   adj. 一年两次的
7. recalibrate   v. 重新校准
8. tacitly   adv. 肃静地,沉默地
9. peg   n. 钉;桩;借口
        vt. 钉木桩;钩
        vi. 努力工作;匆忙走
        adj. 上宽下窄的
10. expansionary   adj. 扩张性的
11. stance   n. 态度;站立姿势
12. revenue   n. 税收;收入;税务局
13. envisage   vt. 面对;想象
14. sustainability   n. 持续性,能维持性;可持续性
15. stimulus   n. 刺激(物);激励(物)
16. surplus   n. 过剩,剩余,剩余额;盈余,顺差

Useful Expressions

1. fiscal stance 财政态势
2. sustainable growth 可持续增长
3. macroeconomic policy 宏观经济政策
4. interest rates 利率
5. monetary policy 货币政策

Difficult Sentences

1. "This macroeconomic policy mix is assessed to be appropriate given current economic conditions," the central bank said in its latest biannual report, while reaffirming that, "should the outlook for inflation and growth weaken significantly, MAS is prepared to recalibrate monetary policy".

本句中 should the outlook...weaken 作为虚拟倒装省略句,省略了 if,把 should 提到主语之前表示假设条件,主句为:MAS is prepared to recalibrate monetary policy。

译文:"这一宏观经济政策的融合被认为是适合现今经济情况的,如果通货膨胀与经济增长的前景急剧削弱,新加坡金融管理局就准备重新校准金融政策。"

2. This year's expansionary fiscal impulse - which means that the government has taken out less revenue than it is spending, against the year before - follows initiatives from a "longer - term sustainable growth" budget that the MAS noted were meant to raise productivity and tackle social inequality.

本句两个破折号之间是 which 引导的定语从句,主句是 This year's expansionary fiscal impulse follows initiatives from a "longer - term sustainable growth" budget。"that the MAS noted were meant to raise productivity and tackle social inequality" 是 budget 后面所跟的定语从句。

译文：今年扩大化的财政刺激遵循了一项长期持续性增长的财政预算新方案，这意味着相对于去年来说，政府会拿出更少的税收，花更多的经费，这一项由金融管理局提出的财政预算方案是为了提高生产力并处理社会不均衡现象。

Reading Comprehension

There are five statements attached to the passage containing information given in one of the paragraphs. Identify the paragraph from which the information is derived and each paragraph is marked with a letter. You may only choose one paragraph once. Write down the letter in the blanks of each statement.

_____ 1. The medium-term target of Singapore's economic development is to seek price stability and sustainable growth.

_____ 2. One of the most important differences between Singapore and other economies lies in the central bank's usage of the Singdollar exchange rate.

_____ 3. The range of the expected economic growth has been slowed down when Singapore Budget attempted to be slightly stimulatory.

_____ 4. The MAS claimed that the economic slowdown in the past six months in Singapore was more severe when its trade-related sectors were less anticipated.

_____ 5. The central bank considered the macroeconomic policy mix was just conforming to the present economic situations.

Reading and Discussion

1. What are the main economic target that Singapore is trying to achieve today?
2. What does 2019's expansionary fiscal impulse suggest?
3. According to the MAS, what may restrain the stimulus to economies?

Language in Use

Complete each sentence with a word listed below. Make changes where necessary.

| reiterate   stimulatory   expansionary   revenue   sustainability |

1. The Monetary Authority of Singapore _____ that it would continue to loose its monetary policy this year.

2. An _____ fiscal policy would be carried out in Singapore to maintain a better long-term economic development.

3. Unlike last year, the Singapore government took out less _____ than its spending in the coming year.

4. The target of economic growth is to reach the _____ in debt and stablity in finance.

5. The government in Singapore worked with efforts to keep its budget mildly _____.

Reading 3
Vietnam Passes Cybersecurity Law Despite Privacy Concerns
撇开隐私顾虑，越南通过网络安全法案

June 11, 2018 (*The Associated Press*)

A　Vietnamese legislators on Tuesday passed a contentious cybersecurity law, which critics say will hurt the economy and further restrict freedom of expression.

B　The law requires service providers such as Google and Facebook to store user data in Vietnam, open offices in the country and remove offending contents within 24 hours at the request of the Ministry of Information and Communications and the specialized cybersecurity task-force under the Ministry of Public Security.

C　Viet said the law doesn't contradict Vietnam's commitments to multinational trade treaties such as the World Trade Organization and the Trans-Pacific Partnership, but he said there are exceptions on national security grounds.

D　He said requiring foreign companies to set up data centers in Vietnam may increase their operational costs, but it was necessary for the country's cybersecurity and will facilitate the companies' operations and user activities.

E　Jeff Paine, managing director of Asia Internet Coalition, an industry association that includes Google and Facebook, said that the group was disappointed with the passage of the law whose requirements on data localization, content control and local offices will hinder the country's ambitions to achieve GDP and job growth.

F　The Vietnam Digital Communications Association said the law may reduce GDP growth by 1.7 percent and wipe out foreign investment by 3.1 percent.

G　The U.S. Embassy said last week it found the draft containing "serious obstacles to Vietnam's cybersecurity and digital innovation future, and may not be consistent with Vietnam's international trade commitments."

H　Amnesty International said the decision has potentially devastating consequences for freedom of expression.

I　"In the country's deeply repressive climate, the online space was a relative refuge where people could go to share ideas and opinions with less fear of censure by the authorities," Clare Algar, Amnesty International's director of global operations, said in a statement Tuesday.

J　"This law can only work if tech companies cooperate with government demands to hand over private data. These companies must not be party to human rights abuses, and we urge them to use the considerable power they have at their disposal to challenge Viet Nam's government on this regressive legislation." she said.

K　Despite sweeping economic reforms since the mid-1980s that made Vietnam one of fastest growing economies in the region, authorities maintains tight control over almost all aspects of life including the media and religion and tolerate no challenge to the one-party rule.

(417 words)

Notes

1. Ministry of Information and Communications：信息和通信部。主管越南各类电子信息的传播、传播媒介与设备及相关法令的制定。
2. Ministry of Public Security：公安部。主管越南公共信息传播的安全与相关措施的制定。
3. World Trade Organization：世界贸易组织。现代最重要的国际经济组织之一，到目前为止，拥有164个成员国，有"经济联合国"之称。
4. Trans-Pacific Partnership Agreement：跨太平洋战略经济伙伴关系协定。是目前重要的国际多边经济谈判组织，由亚太经济合作组织成员国中的新西兰、新加坡、智利和文莱四国发起，原名亚太自由贸易区，旨在促进亚太地区的贸易自由化。
5. Vietnam Digital Communications Association：越南电子通信联合会。民间电子通信企业商会组织。
6. Amnesty International：国际特赦组织。1961年在伦敦成立的世界性民间人权组织。

Words

1. cybersecurity   n. 网络安全
2. contentious   adj. 好辩的，好争吵的；有争议的
3. treaty   n. 条约；协定
4. operational   adj. 操作的，运作的；可用的；作战的
5. facilitate   vt. 促进；帮助；使……容易
6. localization   n. 局限；地方化
7. repressive   adj. 镇压的；压制的
8. refuge   n. 避难，庇护；避难所
           v. 寻求庇护，避难
9. censure   n. 责难，非难
           vt. 非难；责备
           vi. 进行指责
10. legislation   n. 法律；法规；立法

Useful Expressions

1. multinational trade treaties 多国贸易条约
2. operational costs 经营费用
3. data localization 数据本地化储存
4. regressive legislation 倒退性立法

Difficult Sentences

1. The law requires service providers such as Google and Facebook to store user data in Vietnam, open offices in the country and remove offending contents within 24

hours at the request of the Ministry of Information and Communications and the specialized cybersecurity task-force under the Ministry of Public Security.

本句谓语动词较多,其主句为:The law requires service providers... to store user data..., open offices... and remove offending contents....

译文:依据信息和通信部与公安部的专门负责网络安全的特别小组的要求,这条法令规定诸如谷歌、脸书这种服务供应商在越南存储用户数据,需设置办事处并在二十四小时内删除违法信息。

2. Jeff Paine, managing director of Asia Internet Coalition, an industry association that includes Google and Facebook, said that the group was disappointed with the passage of the law whose requirements on data localization, content control and local offices will hinder the country's ambitions to achieve GDP and job growth.

本句用 whose 引导了一个表示所有格的定语从句"whose requirements on data localization, content control and local offices will hinder the country's ambitions to achieve GDP and job growth"来修辞 the law,主句是 Jeff Paine... said that the group was disappointed with the passage of the law。

译文:亚洲互联网联盟——一个包括谷歌和脸书公司在内的工业联合会,其执行董事杰夫·佩恩声明联盟对于此项法令的通过非常失望,这项法案对数据土地化储存、内容控制与设置当地办事处的要求将会阻碍整个国家对 GDP 与就业率的增长的追求。

Reading Comprehension

There are five statements attached to the passage containing information given in one of the paragraphs. Identify the paragraph from which the information is derived and each paragraph is marked with a letter. You may only choose one paragraph once. Write down the letter in the blanks of each statement.

_____ 1. The online space is a place where people could share their ideas without worrying too much about the censure by the authorities.

_____ 2. The requirements for foreign companies to establish data centers in Vietnam might result in a rise in the expenses of operation.

_____ 3. The U.S. Embassy commented on the law draft that it didn't act in accordance with the international trade commitments made by Vietnam.

_____ 4. Vietnam's government holds tight control over the media and religion.

_____ 5. The cybersecurity law said that user's data should be stored in Vietnam by the foreign service providers and offending contents removed in one day.

Reading and Discussion

1. What are the negative effects that the cybersecurity law may bring?
2. Why did Viet consider the law is necessary for the country?
3. What did Clare Algar suggest the tech companies do on the legislation?

Chapter 3 Economy 经济

>>> Language in Use

Complete each sentence with a word listed below. Make changes where necessary.

| treaty   facilitate   localization   refuge   censure |

1. The Vietnam government set a law to make cyber data _____ legalized.

2. The cybersecurity law is said to _____ foreign service providers's operation and protect the nation's cyber environment.

3. The cyberspace is usually regarded as a _____ for the netizens to share their opinions.

4. The foreign cyber service providers considered that the new law had violated the commitments of Vietnam to the international trade _____.

5. The _____ by the authorities is often publicized on national newspapers.

Chapter 4 Society

社会

ASEAN

Reading 1

Man arrested in Singapore Changi Airport for buying ticket just to wave his wife off at the gate
男子在新加坡樟宜机场被捕,只因买机票送妻子到登机口

September 3, 2019(CNN)

A With an on-site butterfly dome, cactus garden and four-story slide, Singapore's Changi airport regularly tops rankings of the best airports in the world.

B But some travelers are taking a little too much of a shine to it.

C The Singapore Police Force has issued a warning to residents not to "misuse" their boarding passes after a man was arrested for buying a ticket to walk his wife to the gate.

D The misuse of boarding passes is an offense in Singapore, where transit areas are considered "protected places."

E Anyone accessing the gate-side areas at Changi without intending to fly can be prosecuted under Singapore's Infrastructure Protection Act and fined up to S＄20,000 (US＄14,300) or imprisoned for up to two years. Thirty three people have been arrested under the legislation in the first eight months of 2019.

F Police said the 27-year-old bought a ticket purely to walk his wife to the gate and had "no intention to depart Singapore."

G In a Facebook post they added that "passengers who enter the transit areas with a boarding pass should only be there for the purpose of traveling to their next destination."

H If the idea that anyone would actively want to spend time in an airport sounds odd, you haven't flown through Singapore.

I When Changi's new Jewel terminal opened in April, it made headlines around the globe for its 40-meter waterfall (the world's largest indoor one), a 14,000-square-meter Canopy Park, complete with a suspension bridge, topiary and mazes, and one of Asia's largest indoor gardens with 3,000 trees and 60,000 shrubs.

J Overstaying your welcome in the terminal is a thing, here.

K In 2016, a Malaysian man was jailed after he spent 18 days in Changi, forging boarding passes to gain entry to nine airport lounges. Shortly afterward, a couple was arrested for booking flexible tickets to gain access to the Changi shopping mall, where they bought an iPhone 7.

L Other passengers have been known to book refundable tickets which they cancel before the flight takes off, having enjoyed the airport.

(387 words)

>>> Notes

1. Changi Airport:樟宜机场,曾多次被知名媒体评为"世界最佳机场",同时也是"旅客票选最佳机场"与"排名第一的全球最佳机场"。

2. boarding pass:登机牌,机场为乘坐航班的乘客提供的登机凭证。登机牌上的信息有姓名、航班号、电子客票号码、乘机日期、登机口的位置、登机时间、座位号码、舱位等级、始发地和目的地。

3. transit area:过境区,国际航班乘客中转等待区。

4. Infrastructure Protection Act:《基础设施保护法》,此法令于2018年12月18日生效。在新加坡,未经授权对军营和关卡等任何敏感设施和地点进行拍摄或录像都是违法的。这些地方的授权人员有权查问可疑人物及检查其随身物品,删除任何违法拍下的照片和影像,也可命令对方离开现场。

5. Facebook:脸书,一家社交网站,可在上面展示个人信息,与人交流等。

6. Jewel terminal:宝石航站楼,位于樟宜机场内,是一个有餐饮、酒店、花园、景点等多功能的航站楼。

7. Canopy Park:星空花园,其占地面积为14000平方米,拥有七个标志性的游乐设施,由来自英国、法国、德国、新加坡和荷兰的顶级设计师们联袂打造,包括镜子迷宫(Mirror Maze)、树篱迷宫(Hedge Maze)、宏利天空之网(Manulife Sky Nets)、奇幻滑梯(Discovery Slides)、天悬桥(Canopy Bridge)、汇丰银行雨漩涡(HSBC Rain Vortex)与资生堂森林谷(Shiseido Forest Valley)全部景点都充满特色。

Words

1. on-site 在工地的;在现场的
2. dome n. 穹顶,穹顶建筑
3. cactus n. 仙人掌
4. offense n. 犯罪行为,罪行
5. access n. 通道,途径;接近(或进入)的机会,权利
   vt. 访问,存取(计算机文件);接近,进入
6. prosecute vt. 起诉;检举
   vi. 起诉;告发
7. legislation n. 法律;立法
8. post n. 邮件;帖子
   adv. 急速地
   vt. 张贴广告
9. odd adj. 奇怪的,古怪的;奇数的;剩余的
   n. 奇特的事物
10. topiary n. 林木修剪(术)
    adj. 修剪成形的
11. maze n. 曲径,迷宫;混乱,糊涂
12. shrub n. 灌木
13. forge vt. 锻造、伪造(货币、文件等),假冒(签名)
    vi. 做铁匠,干伪造勾当
    n. 锻铁炉
14. lounge n. (酒店、机场、剧院等的)休息厅,等候室

vi. (懒洋洋地)倚

vt. 吊儿郎当地消磨(时间)

Useful Expressions

1. take a shine to 喜欢上,有好感
2. suspension bridge 悬索桥,吊桥
3. flexible ticket 可改签机票
4. refundable ticket 可退机票

Difficult Sentences

1. With an on-site butterfly dome, cactus garden and four-story slide, Singapore's Changi airport regularly tops rankings of the best airports in the world.

本句中 regularly 表示经常地,top 用作动词表示"为……之首"。With 短语表示伴随,作状语。

译文:新加坡樟宜机场是世界名列前茅的最佳机场,拥有蝶形穹顶、仙人掌花园以及四层滑梯。

2. Anyone accessing the gate-side areas at Changi without intending to fly can be prosecuted under Singapore's Infrastructure Protection Act and fined up to S＄20,000 (US＄14,300) or imprisoned for up to two years.

本句中 accessing the gate-side areas at Changi without intending to fly 作后置定语修饰 anyone。

译文:根据新加坡《基础设施保护法》,任何无意登机而进入樟宜机场登机口区域的人都可能被起诉,并被处以最高2万新元(约合1.43万美元)的罚款,或最长两年的监禁。

3. Overstaying your welcome in the terminal is a thing, here.

本句中短语 overstay your welcome 表示待得太久而不再受欢迎,a thing 在这里指事情,表示强调。

译文:在这个机场长时间逗留已经成为一种现象。

Reading Comprehension

There are five statements attached to the passage containing information given in one of the paragraphs. Identify the paragraph from which the information is derived and each paragraph is marked with a letter. You may only choose one paragraph once. Write down the letter in the blanks of each statement.

_____ 1. Anyone going to the boarding area but not wanting to board a flight could face a fine or even imprisoned.

_____ 2. The people in Singapore were warned by the police that their boarding passes should not be used incorrectly and carelessly.

_____ 3. Some travelers think the airport is very attractive to them.

_____ 4. If you have never been to Chanqi's new Jewel terminal you must think it is a very strange idea for desiring to stay there.

_____ 5. Changqi's new Jewel terminal got a lot of worldwide publicity from the media for the world's largest indoor waterfall, a 14,000-square-meter Canopy Park, a suspension bridge, topiary and mazes, and one of Asia's largest indoor gardens.

Questions for Discussion

1. What is the warning that the Singapore Police Force has issued?
2. Why can't people misuse their boarding passes in Singapore?
3. Why did Jewel terminal make headlines around the globe?

Language in Use

Complete each sentence with a word listed below. Make changes where necessary.

on-site   legislation   forge   offense   odd

1. A number of _____ works of art have been sold as genuine.
2. It's the third time that he's been convicted of a drug _____.
3. It must be _____ to go back to your hometown after forty years away.
4. Several governments have adopted tough new anti-terrorist _____ in the wake of the attacks.
5. We're meeting the contractor _____ tomorrow.

Reading 2

Trash for tickets on Indonesia's "plastic bus"
回收垃圾出奇招：印度尼西亚推出"塑料公交车"

August 9, 2019(AFP)

A Dozens of people clutching bags full of plastic bottles and disposable cups queue at a busy bus terminal in the Indonesian city of Surabaya — where passengers can swap trash for travel tickets.

B The nation is the world's second-biggest marine polluter and has pledged to reduce plastic waste in its waters some 70 percent by 2025 by boosting recycling, raising public awareness, and curbing usage. The Surabaya Scheme has been a hit in the city of 2.9 million, with nearly 16,000 passengers trading trash for free travel each week, according to authorities.

C "This is a very smart solution. It's free and instead of throwing away bottles people now collect them and bring them here," explains 48-year-old resident Fransiska Nugrahepi. An hour-long bus ride with unlimited stops costs three large bottles, five medium bottles or 10 plastic cups. But they must be cleaned and cannot be squashed.

D Franki Yuanus, a Surabaya transport official, says the programme aims not only to cut waste but also to tackle traffic congestion by encouraging people to switch to public transit. "There has been a good response from the public," insists Yuanus, adding, "Paying with plastic is one of the things that has made people enthusiastic because up until now plastic waste was just seen as useless."

E Currently the fleet consists of 20 near-new buses, each with recycling bins and ticket officers who roam the aisles to collect any leftover bottles. Authorities said roughly six tons of plastic rubbish are collected from passengers each month before being auctioned to recycling companies.

F Nurhayati Anwar, who uses the bus about once a week with her three-year-old son, said the trash swap programme is changing how people see their throwaway cups and bottles. "Now people in the office or at home are trying to collect (rubbish) instead of just throwing it away," the 44-year-old accountant told AFP after trading in several bottles for a free ride, "We now know that plastic is not good for the environment — people in Surabaya are starting to learn."

G Other parts of Indonesia, an archipelago of some 17,000 islands, are also trying to tackle the issue. Bali is phasing in a ban on single-use plastic straws and bags to rid the popular holiday island of waste choking its waterways, while authorities in the capital Jakarta are considering a similar bylaw to rid the city of plastic shopping bags.

H Governments around the globe are increasingly taking measures to curb the menace of disposable plastic.

J A 2016 report by the Ellen MacArthur Foundation warned there would be more plastic than fish, by weight, in the seas by 2050.

K It estimated eight million tonnes of plastics enter oceans annually.

L It added: "This is equivalent to dumping the contents of one garbage truck into the ocean every minute. If no action is taken, this is expected to increase to two per minute by 2030 and four per minute by 2050."

(508 words)

Notes

1. Surabaya:泗水,印尼城市名,印尼第二大城市。
2. AFP:法新社,法国新闻社的简称。
3. Bali:巴厘岛,印尼著名的旅游胜地。
4. Jakarta(the capital and largest city of Indonesia):雅加达,印尼首都及最大城市。

Words

1. clutch   vt. 紧握
          vi. 企图抓住
          n. 一群人(或物)
2. marine adj. 海(洋)的;航海的;海运的
          n. (一个国家的)所有船舶

3. pledge   n. 誓言;诺言;保证
            vi. 发誓;保证
            vt. 许诺

4. curb   vt. 控制,约束,抑制
          n. 控制

5. hit   n. 非常受欢迎的人(或事);非常成功的人(或事)
         vt. 打击,迎合
         vi. 打击,碰撞

6. squash   vt. 把……压扁;把……挤扁
            vi. 被压碎

7. transit   n. 运输;输送
             vi. 通过

8. fleet   n. (统一指挥下的或在一起活动的)船队,车队,机群;海军
           adj. 快速的
           vi. 疾飞,掠过
           vt. 消磨(时间)

9. roam   vi. 闲逛(于);漫步(于)
          vt. 在……随便走
          n. 漫步

10. aisle   n. 走廊,过道

11. auction   vt. 拍卖
              n. 拍卖

12. swap   vt. 交换,交易
           vi. 进行交换
           n. 交换(物),交易(物)

13. archipelago   n. 群岛;多岛屿的海

14. phase   vt. 分阶段实施,逐步进行
            vi. 分阶段(或逐步)前进
            n. 阶段,时期

15. choke   v. (使)窒息,(使)哽噎;堵塞,阻塞;抑制(感情)

16. bylaw   n. 地方法

17. disposable   adj. 一次性的,用后可扔掉的

18. equivalent   adj. 相等的;等价的

Useful Expressions

1. raising public awareness 提高公众意识
2. traffic congestion 交通拥堵
3. trade in 买卖,抵价购物

Chapter 4　Society 社会

>>> **Difficult Sentences**

1. The Surabaya Scheme has been a hit in the city of 2.9 million, with nearly 16,000 passengers trading trash for free travel each week, according to authorities.

本句中 with nearly 16,000...authorities 是独立主格结构，作句子的伴随状语。

译文：印尼有关部门称，"泗水计划"在这座有着290万人口的城市大受欢迎，每周有近1.6万名乘客用垃圾换车票。

2. Currently the fleet consists of 20 near-new buses, each with recycling bins and ticket officers who roam the aisles to collect any leftover bottles.

本句中 fleet 表示车队，roam 表示来回走动。with 结构作状语。

译文：目前，车队由20辆几乎全新的巴士组成，每辆巴士都配有回收箱和检票员，检票员会在车厢过道里来回走动，收集剩余的瓶子。

3. Bali is phasing in a ban on single-use plastic straws and bags to rid the popular holiday island of waste choking its waterways, while authorities in the capital Jakarta are considering a similar bylaw to rid the city of plastic shopping bags.

本句中 phase in 短语表示逐步采用，single-use 表示一次性的，choking 表示堵塞。

译文：巴厘岛正逐步禁止使用一次性塑料吸管和塑料袋，以清除这个度假胜地的岛屿上堵塞水道的垃圾。与此同时，首都雅加达的有关部门也在考虑制定类似的法规，以清除该市的塑料购物袋。

>>> **Reading Comprehension**

There are five statements attached to the passage containing information given in one of the paragraphs. Identify the paragraph from which the information is derived and each paragraph is marked with a letter. You may only choose one paragraph once. Write down the letter in the blanks of each statement.

_____ 1. Indonesia, ranks the second on sea pollution, has promised to eliminate 70 percent of plastic waste in its water area through promoting recycling and public awareness and restricted usage.

_____ 2. A transport official expressed that the program did not merely reduce waste, furthermore it encouraged people riding on public transportation, and consequently solved traffic congestion.

_____ 3. In order to eliminate the garbage that blocked the waterways of the famous holiday resort, Bali is in successive steps to ban the single-use plastic straws and bags.

_____ 4. At present, there is a fleet consisting 20 practically new buses which are equipped with recycling bins and ticket-takers collecting used bottles.

_____ 5. A mother of a 3-year-old son made comment that the trash swap programme gradually changes people's opinion about their throwaway cups and bottles.

Reading and Discussion

1. What does Indonesia promise to do as the world's second-biggest marine country?

2. How can people pay for their bus ride for an hour?

3. Are there other measures mentioned in the news in order to get rid of wastes? What are they?

Language in Use

Complete each sentence with a word listed below. Make changes where necessary.

transit   equivalent   phase   pledge   roam

1. The reduction in armed forces will be _____ over the next ten years.

2. The question is whether road _____ is cheaper than rail.

3. Here's the give-away, a pair of tusks two meters long, the trademark of a Columbian mammoth, the biggest animal to _____ the ice age plains.

4. But Mr. Bush made no _____ on the size of emissions cuts that the US would be prepared to sign up to and gave no indication of a timeframe.

5. It needs to rein in its defense spending, which is currently _____ to that of the next 20 countries combined.

Reading 3

Smoking inside a house equals to "domestic violence"
泰国控烟出新招 在家吸烟将视作"家暴"

August 22, 2019 (*China Daily*)

A Smoking in your own home in Thailand may now be considered a crime, if the smoke is considered harmful to other people in the house.

B The new law, Family Protection and Development Promotion Act, was initiated by the Ministry of Social Development and Human Security and was announced in the Royal Gazette on May 22, 2019.

C The law aims at curbing smoking at home which might be hazardous for others' health residing under the same roof. In that case, it will be considered as "domestic violence". The new law came into force on August 20.

D According to the center for research and knowledge management for tobacco control, at the Faculty of Medical Science of Mahidol University, there are about 4.9 million households where one or more family members smoke.

E An average of 10.3 million people have unwittingly become passive smokers because they've been inhaling smoke at home. Scientific studies show that passive smokers are at greater risk of being affected by cancer.

F Of 75 child patients from houses where smoking is practiced, 76% of them were found to have nicotine traces in their urine, with 43% of them having nicotine content exceeding permissible levels.

G Smoking at home also "may lead to physical or emotional violence" because of aggressiveness when there is a lack of smoking, and might as well ruin relationships between smokers and non-smoker family members.

H According to the new law, anyone who thinks they are affected by domestic smoking can report to officials concerned so that inspectors will be sent to investigate and take legal action against the smokers.

I Once convicted, the court may order a person to receive treatment to quit smoking in an attempt to protect the person's family.

J In February this year, Thailand had banned smoking at six of its airports along with a ban in public places.

(316 words)

Notes

1. Royal Gazette:《皇家公报》,泰国一家有影响力的报纸。
2. Faculty of Medical Science of Mahidol University:玛希隆大学医学院。玛希隆大学是泰国最古老的高等教育机构,在医学、公共医疗卫生和自然科学领域享有盛誉。它起源于在1888年成立的诗里拉医院。在1943年,正式成立并命名为医科大学,于1969年以"泰国现代医学和公共医疗卫生事业之父"——玛希隆·阿杜德(Mahidol of Songkla)王子的名字命名。
3. nicotine:尼古丁,烟碱,是一种存在于茄科植物(茄属)中的生物碱,也是烟草的重要成分。

Words

1. initiate n. 被传授初步知识的人
             vt. 开始,创始,发起
             adj. 被传授初步知识的
2. hazardous adj. 有危险的
3. reside v. 居住,定居
4. household n. 一家人,一户,家庭
5. unwittingly adv. 糊里糊涂地,茫然地;无意地
6. inhale vt. 吸气;吸入
           n. 吸入
           vi. 吸入气体
7. trace n. 痕迹,踪迹;微量,少许
8. urine n. 尿液,小便
9. content n. 目录;内容;容量
10. exceed vt. 超过,超出

vi. 占优势,突出
11. aggressiveness　n. 积极主动;进攻性
12. inspector　n. 检查员;视察员;巡官
13. convict　v. 宣判……有罪,证明……有罪
14. court　n. 法院,法庭
　　　　　vt. 追求,企图获得
　　　　　vi. 求婚
　　　　　adj. 法庭的

Useful Expressions

1. domestic violence 家庭暴力
2. come into force 生效
3. passive smokers 被动吸烟者
4. exceed permissible levels 超出允许的范围

Difficult Sentences

1. The law aims at curbing smoking at home which might be hazardous for others' health residing under the same roof.

本句中 curb smoking 表示限制吸烟,which 从句修饰 smoking at home。

译文:这项法律旨在限制在家中吸烟的行为,这种行为可能会伤害家中共同生活的其他家庭成员的健康。

2. Smoking at home also "may lead to physical or emotional violence" because of aggressiveness when there is a lack of smoking, and might as well ruin relationships between smokers and non-smoker family members.

might as well 表示(反正也没有更好的办法)要不就……,when 引导的是时间状语。

译文:在家吸烟也"可能导致身体或情绪暴力",因为在吸不到烟时,吸烟者可能产生攻击性,进而破坏吸烟者和非吸烟者家庭成员之间的关系。

3. According to the new law, anyone who thinks they are affected by domestic smoking can report to officials concerned so that inspectors will be sent to investigate and take legal action against the smokers.

本句中 who 引导的是定语从句,修饰限制 anyone。

译文:根据这项新法律,任何认为自己受到家庭成员吸烟影响的人都可以向有关官员报告,以便政府派检查员调查并对吸烟者采取法律行动。

Reading Comprehension

There are five statements attached to the passage containing information given in one of the paragraphs. Identify the paragraph from which the information is derived and each paragraph is marked with a letter. You may only choose one paragraph once. Write down the letter in the blanks of each statement.

Chapter 4 Society 社会

_____ 1. Thailand had placed a ban on smoking at six airports and in public in this February.

_____ 2. As long as declared to be guilty, smokers will be forced to be treated in order to get rid of smoking, and their family can be protected.

_____ 3. In Thailand if the smoker who smokes even in his own house may does harm to other family members, he will be convicted guilty.

_____ 4. Because they can't smoke, smokers may become aggressive and accordingly hurt the relationship between family members.

_____ 5. Averagely, 10.3 million people are not aware of becoming passive smokers who may face greater risk of cancer as a result of secondhand smoking.

》》》 Reading and Discussion

1. When did the law against smoking at home come into force?
2. Why does scientists think it is harmful to become a passive smoker?
3. What punishment will smokers get if they violate the new law?

》》》 Language in Use

Complete each sentence with a word listed below. Make changes where necessary.

exceed   unwittingly   initiate   convict   reside

1. Being new with the company, I had to quickly get my feet on the ground and _____ a plan.

2. Officials said the average price of tobacco in the ongoing auction in Karnataka is going to _____ the record price soon.

3. In just a few months our tools have been installed by over 200,000 people, most of which _____ in the United States.

4. If _____, she could be jailed for five years for living off immoral earnings.

5. You might _____ imply that you're going to ask for a raise soon after coming on board.

Chapter 5 Science and Technology

科学和技术

ASEAN

Chapter 5　Science and Technology 科学和技术

Reading 1

5G takes centre stage with various tech demos
各种 5G 技术演示成为瞩目焦点

October 29, 2019 (*Bangkok Post*)

A　Enthusiasm for the 5G wireless network is heightening with an array of related use cases, Internet of Things (IoT) and artificial intelligence (AI) technologies that capitalize on the ultra-fast Internet, all on display at Digital Thailand Big Bang 2019.

B　The event, jointly hosted by the Digital Economy Promotion Agency and the Digital Economy and Society Ministry, began yesterday and runs until Thursday at BITEC, Bangna.

C　5G deployment is expected to start next year, with experiments building up business use cases, while full competition in 5G business is expected by 2021.

D　Drones, remote-controlled vehicles, robotics, smart homes, smart factories, smart farms and smart healthcare are expected to be the first tier of 5G use cases, according to analysts.

E　"We are fully committed to a 5G network in Thailand as it will go beyond connectivity and business productivity and use cases, giving consumers access to innovative public services." said Alexandra Reich, chief executive of Total Access Communications (DTAC), at the event.

F　She said DTAC wants to see a clear frequency roadmap, particularly regarding frequency availability, from authorities.

G　"Auction pricing is important as 5G network investment carries a very high cost," said Ms Reich. "Some US＄2.4 trillion is expected to be spent on the 5G network globally in 2020."

H　"The telecom regulator may have to consider providing financial assistance for mobile operators or introducing an infrastructure-sharing scheme for mobile operators or introducing an infrastructure-sharing scheme to ease the financial burden shouldered by operators." she said.

I　DTAC is preparing AI and digital innovation teams that would cater to business use cases for 5G services and take steps to work out the frequency auction plan.

J　The company plans to offer 5G Fixed Wireless Access Internet service under its DTAC@Home project, competing with the fibre-optic high-speed network. The service offers a minimum speed of 15 megabits per second.

K　Somchai Lertsutiwong, chief executive of Advanced Info Service (AIS), said the company is committed to providing 5G for Thais.

L　At the event, AIS displayed video calling across provinces through 5G networks for the first time. Remote-controlled vehicles using 5G were also demonstrated.

M　True Corporation chief Suphachai Chearavanont said 5G network deployment is expected by the end of next year, making Thailand an early 5G adopter in ASEAN.

N Chinese tech giant Huawei demonstrated how 5G networks help transform business models in a wide range of sectors, including industry, daily life, AI services and 3D reconstruction.

O Visitors can also experience manoeuvring drones brought from Qingdao, China and watch HD video filmed by the drones.

(415 words)

Notes

1. Digital Thailand Big Bang 2019：2019泰国数字"Big Bang"展览会以"ASEAN Connectivity"为主题，本次活动将成为国际与东盟国家在经济、社会、文化、技术、创新等领域建立合作和网络的平台。它是整个东南亚地区最大的ICT展，也是泰国及东盟地区最具影响力的展会之一。

2. Digital Economy Promotion Agency：数字经济促进会，缩写为DEPA。其目标是使泰国成为亚洲物联网中心，推动东盟的数字化。

3. Digital Economy and Society Ministry：泰国数字经济与社会部。它管理的部门和公司有信息和通信技术部、国家统计局、软件产业促进局、电子交易发展局、泰国气象局、泰国邮政，以及国有电信公司TOT和CAT电信等。

4. BITEC：(Bangkok International Trade & Exhibition Centre)：曼谷国际贸易展览中心，是一个世界级的会议和展览场所，位于曼谷市。

Words

1. enthusiasm n. 热情；热心；热忱；热衷的事物
2. array n. 大堆，大群，大量；数组，阵列；排列
         vt. 排列；配置(兵力)
3. artificial adj. 人工的，人造的；假的
4. intelligence n. 智力，才智，智慧
5. jointly adv. 连带地，共同地
6. deployment n. (部队、资源或装备的)部署，调集
7. drone n. 嗡嗡声；持续低音；雄蜂；无人机
         vi. 嗡嗡叫，嗡嗡响
         vt. 低沉单调地说
8. tier n. 阶层；等级
         vt. 层层排列；使层叠成递升排列；层叠
         vi. 成递升排列
9. connectivity n. 连接(度)，联结(度)；联系
10. access n. 通道，通路，入径；(使用或见到的)机会，权利
           vt. 访问，存取(计算机文件)；到达，进入
11. innovative adj. 引进新思想的；革新的，创新的
12. road map n. 道路图
13. authority n. 权力；当权(地位)；当局；权威

Chapter 5　Science and Technology　科学和技术

14. tion　n. v. 拍卖
15. infrastructure　n. （国家或机构的）基础设施
16. cater　vt. （为社交活动）提供饮食，承办（酒席）；
    vi. 迎合；承办酒席
17. fibre-optic　adj. 光学纤维的
18. megabit　n. 兆比特，兆位（等于100万比特）
19. transform　vt. 使改变形态；使改变外观
20. manoeuvre　n. 细致巧妙的移动；机动动作；策略，花招，伎俩；军事演习，作战演习
    vi. 进行演习；用策略
    vt. 调动，使演习；诱使；（敏捷或巧妙地）操纵

Useful Expressions

1. be expected to 期望；预计；有望做某事
2. be committed to 投入；承担；致力于；完全旨在
3. take steps to 采取措施

Difficult Sentences

1. Enthusiasm for the 5G wireless network is heightening with an array of related use cases, Internet of Things (IoT) and artificial intelligence (AI) technologies that capitalize on the ultra-fast Internet, all on display at Digital Thailand Big Bang 2019.

本句中 Internet of Things 指物联网，artificial intelligence 指人工智能，capitalize on 指充分利用某事物。

译文：随着一系列相关使用实例、物联网（IoT）和人工智能（AI）技术在利用了超高速互联网后得以实现，人们对5G无线网络的热情日益高涨，这些技术均在2019年数字泰国大爆炸展会上展出。

2. "The telecom regulator may have to consider providing financial assistance for mobile operators or introducing an infrastructure-sharing scheme for mobile operators or introducing an infrastructure-sharing scheme to ease the financial burden shouldered by operators." she said.

本句中"shouldered by operators"放在所修饰名词"burden"的后面作后置定语，我们也可将这一后置定语改为定语从句"which is shouldered by operators"。

译文：她表示，电信监管机构可能必须考虑向移动运营商提供财政援助，或向移动运营商推出基础设施共享计划，或推出可以减轻运营商财政负担的基础设施共享计划。

Reading Comprehension

There are five statements attached to the passage containing information given in one of the paragraphs. Identify the paragraph from which the information is derived and each paragraph is marked with a letter. You may only choose one paragraph once. Write down the letter in the blanks of each statement.

_____ 1. According to True Corporation chief Suphachai Chearavanont, it is expected that 5G network will be deployed by the end of next year.

_____ 2. Alexandra Reich, chief executive of Total Access Communications, said DTAC would like to see a clear frequency guide from authorities.

_____ 3. Chinese tech company Huawei took part in the Digital Thailand Big Bang 2019 and displayed some related use cases.

_____ 4. With the emergence of a series of related use cases, IoT and AI technologies, people's enthusiasm for 5G wireless network is growing.

_____ 5. It is estimated that the global 5G network will cost about $2.4 trillion in 2020.

Reading and Discussion

1. What should telecom regulator do to help mobile operators committed to 5G network according to Alexandra Reich, chief executive of Total Access Communications (DTAC)?

2. What will be the first batch of 5G use cases according to analysts?

3. What will DTAC do to compete with the fibre-optic high-speed network?

Language in Use

Complete each sentence with a word listed below. Make changes where necessary.

intelligence   access   innovative   artificial   cater

1. Most of our work now involves _____ for weddings.
2. There will be a prize for the most _____ design.
3. A job interview is a very _____ situation.
4. You've illegally _____ and misused confidential security files.
5. Nerve cells, after all, do not have _____ of their own.

Reading 2

2020 Budget: A boost for Malaysia's tech industry
2020年预算：推动马来西亚科技产业发展

October 14, 2019 (*New Straits Times*)

A KUALA LUMPUR: The 2020 Budget demonstrates that the local technology industry is continuing to get much attention from the government, which is intent on further boosting the capabilities of local SMEs and start-ups, strengthening digital content, embracing digitization, enhancing e-commerce, and adopting 5G technology.

B Local technology players, industry associations and tech agencies in general applaud the various allocations set aside towards making Malaysia a stronger player and contender in the technology arena, both locally and abroad.

C The association representing the information and communications technology (ICT) industry in Malaysia (Pikom) says the Budget puts various short-, medium- and long-term goals in realistic perspective, and paves the way for the unfolding of the Shared Prosperity Vision 2030 (WKB2030).

D Its chairman, Ganesh Kumar Bangah, said the association is pleased to see that there will be special incentives for start-ups to penetrate the world market.

Elevating digital transformation

E Budget 2020 also illustrates that the government is actively encouraging more local businesses to move rapidly into the technology sphere.

F Malaysia Digital Economy Corporation (MDEC) CEO Surina Shukri said all the allocations will empower the digital economy initiatives championed by MDEC, and will directly support the recently-launched WKB2030.

G "The digital transformation agenda for Malaysia continues to be a major catalytic driver for the nation's economy. We are encouraged to note that Budget 2020 includes proposals, which will further accelerate Malaysia's rapidly-maturing digital economy," she said.

H Surina said a new program, called 100 Go Digital, has been launched to enable traditional Malaysian businesses to embrace digitization. This will enable local businesses to fully leverage on digital transformation to address their common pain points.

I She said that under the budget allocation, MDEC will also continue to manage and improve its Digital Transformation Acceleration Program (DTAP).

Digital content boost

J The Government has also allocated RM20 million towards creating a conducive, inclusive, and competitive Digital Content Ecosystem.

K "The Malaysian digital content ecosystem represents an industry that has tremendous export potential, and is greatly reliant on our talent and ingenuity, and resonates very strongly with young Malaysians.

L "With over RM7.6 billion in revenue, a fast-growing RM1.3 billion export revenue and over 10,000 jobs, this industry is poised for the next stage of growth," said Surina. She said the allocation represents another wonderful opportunity for all Malaysians and talented content creators from around the world to continue to build on that success.

M "This move reinforces the confidence that we, as a nation, have for the creative content industry. By increasing opportunities to participate in this industry, Malaysia can, and will, step up its competitive efforts in this space and push the nation as the destination for digital content production."

(436 words)

Notes

1. Kuala Lumpur：马来西亚的首都吉隆坡。吉隆坡是一个对东南亚的文化、教育、体育、财政、经济、商业、金融都具有极大影响力的国际大都会。因许多在东南亚召开的国际外交会议都会在吉隆坡举行，因此吉隆坡也被视为是东南亚外交的两大中心之一。

2. SME(Small and Medium-sized Enterprise)：中小型企业。中小型企业是相对于微型企业而言的生产规模更大的企业，即劳动力、劳动手段、劳动对象和产品生产集中程度高的企业。

3. Shared Prosperity Vision 2030（WKB2030）：10月5日，马来西亚政府在吉隆坡向公众推出了《2030年共享繁荣愿景》（马来语缩写为WKB2030）。该愿景旨在刺激马来西亚经济成长，让全体民众共享经济发展果实。《2030年共享繁荣愿景》提到要将马来西亚低技能劳动密集型经济结构调整为知识型经济结构的十年目标。

4. Malaysia Digital Economy Corporation（MDEC）：马来西亚数字经济发展局是组织和引导马来西亚数字经济发展的机构。

Words

1. budget　n. 预算；政府的年度预算
　　　　　vt. 按计划花(钱)；把……编入预算
　　　　　vi. 编预算
　　　　　adj. 价格低廉的；花钱少的
2. start-up　adj.（新企业）开办阶段的，启动时期的
　　　　　　n. 刚成立的公司，新企业
3. strengthen　vt. 加强，增强，巩固
　　　　　　　vi. 变强
4. embrace　v. 拥抱；欣然接受，乐意采纳（思想、建议等）；信奉（宗教、信仰等）；包括，包含
　　　　　　n. 拥抱，怀抱；接受
5. digitization　n. 数码化；数字化
6. enhance　vt. 提高，增强，增进
　　　　　　vi.（价格等）上涨
7. applaud　vi. 鼓掌，称赞，赞许，赞赏
　　　　　　vt. 向……喝彩；称赞
8. allocation　n. 划拨的款项，分配的东西；分配
9. arena　n. 圆形运动场，圆形剧场；竞争场所；角斗场
10. perspective　n. 态度，观点；洞察力
　　　　　　　　adj. 透视的
11. pave　vt.（用砖石）铺(地)；铺满
12. incentive　n. 激励，刺激，鼓励
　　　　　　　adj. 刺激(性)的

Chapter 5　Science and Technology 科学和技术

13. penetrate　vt. 穿过；进入；渗透，打入（组织、团体等）
　　　　　　　vi. 看透；透过……看见
14. sphere　n. 球，球体，球形，球状物；范围，领域；阶层，界
　　　　　　vt. 形成球体；围绕，置于球面内部
15. empower　v. 授权，给（某人）……的权力，增加（某人的）自主权；使能够，许可
16. catalytic　adj.（化学物质）起催化作用的，有催化性的；促进性的
　　　　　　　n. 催化剂；刺激因素
17. conducive　adj. 有助的，有益的
18. inclusive　adj. 包括的；包括一切费用在内的
19. ecosystem　n. 生态系统，生态圈，生态体系
20. ingenuity　n. 独创力，心灵手巧
21. resonate　vt. 使产生共鸣，使发出回响
　　　　　　vi. 回响；共振
22. revenue　n. 财政收入，税收收入；收益
23. poise　n. 镇定；平静；平稳；姿势
　　　　　vt. 把……拿着不动；使稳定
　　　　　vi. 平衡；悬起；做好准备

Useful Expressions

1. locally and abroad　国内外
2. long-term goals　长期目标
3. digital economy　数字经济
4. digital transformation　数字化改造

Difficult Sentences

1. The 2020 Budget demonstrates that the local technology industry is continuing to get much attention from the government, which is intent on further boosting the capabilities of local SMEs and start-ups, strengthening digital content, embracing digitization, enhancing e-commerce, and adopting 5G technology.

本句中 that 引导的宾语从句做谓语动词 demonstrates 的宾语，which 引导的非限制性定语从句修饰先行词 government。

译文：2020年的预算显示，地方科技产业继续受到政府的高度重视，政府有意进一步提升地方中小型企业和初创企业的能力，加强数字内容，拥抱数字化，加强电子商务，并采用5G技术。

2. The association representing the information and communications technology (ICT) industry in Malaysia (Pikom) says the Budget puts various short-, medium- and long-term goals in realistic perspective, and paves the way for the unfolding of the Shared Prosperity Vision 2030 (WKB2030).

本句中"representing the information and communications technology (ICT) industry in Malaysia (Pikom)"是"association"的后置定语，可改为定语从句"which represents the information and communications technology (ICT) industry in Malaysia (Pikom)".

译文：代表马来西亚信息和通信技术产业的协会（Pikom）表示，该预算从现实角度考虑各种短期、中期和长期目标，并为《2030年共同繁荣愿景》的展开铺平了道路。

3. The Malaysian digital content ecosystem represents an industry that has tremendous export potential, and is greatly reliant on our talent and ingenuity, and resonates very strongly with young Malaysians.

译文：马来西亚的数字内容的生态系统代表着一个具有巨大出口潜力的行业，它在很大程度上依赖于我们的人才和创造力，并与马来西亚年轻人产生了强烈的共鸣。

Reading Comprehension

There are five statements attached to the passage containing information given in one of the paragraphs. Identify the paragraph from which the information is derived and each paragraph is marked with a letter. You may only choose one paragraph once. Write down the letter in the blanks of each statement.

_____ 1. RM20 million will be given by the government to build a competitive digital content ecosystem.

_____ 2. The 2020 Budget is another great chance for all Malaysians and talented content creators around the world to achieve greater success.

_____ 3. The 2020 Budget reveals that the government will continue to attach great importance to the development of local technology industry.

_____ 4. The digital transformation agenda will continue to be the main driving force for Malaysia's economic development.

_____ 5. The various appropriations allocated to make Malaysia a stronger player and competitor in the field of technology at home and abroad are widely praised.

Reading and Discussion

1. What's local technology players attitude towards the budget?
2. What's the purpose of the launch of the program called 100 Go Digital?
3. What will MDEC do under the budget allocation, according to Surina Shukri?

Language in Use

Complete each sentence with a word listed below. Make changes where necessary.

| ecosystem   access   budget   empower   applaud |

1. We decorated the house on a tight _____.
2. She was _____ as she came on stage.
3. His position does not _____ him to cite our views without consultation.
4. The only _____ to the farmhouse is across the fields.
5. Madagascar's _____ range from rainforest to semi-desert.

Reading 3

Alipay, Singapore Tourism Board provide 1st cashless trip for Chinese tourists
支付宝、新加坡旅游局为中国游客提供第一次无现金旅行

September 14, 2018 (Xinhuanet.com)

A Mobile payment company Alipay and the Singapore Tourism Board (STB) on Thursday jointly announced the conclusion of the first cashless trip made by Chinese visitors to Singapore.

B According to a statement from Alipay, the trip was designed to promote Singapore's various destination offerings that accept Alipay's cashless payment platform to demonstrate to Chinese visitors that they can enjoy the same seamless experience in Singapore as they do back at home.

C Six Alipay users were invited by Alipay and the STB to the trip through a social media campaign. During the trip, they used Alipay for purchases including meals, accommodations, transportation, gifts and souvenirs, and entertainment experiences. "We are pleased to have partnered with Alipay in this activity given their strong reach and understanding of the Chinese market, our top source market for both visitor arrivals and tourist spending." said Jacqueline Ng, director of the STB's Marketing Partnerships and Planning, in the press release.

D "We hope to use the insights from this initiative to explore better ways of engaging Chinese visitors and to offer more compelling and seamless experiences through Alipay that are better tailored to their passions." she added.

E Cherry Huang, general manager of Alipay's Cross-border Business for South and Southeast Asia, said, "We are very pleased to work with the STB to provide a cashless experience for Chinese tourists travelling to Singapore. Through Alipay, we hope to help even more merchants in Singapore connect with Chinese tourists."

F Statistics from the STB show visitor arrivals from China to Singapore grew 10 percent year-on-year to around 933,000 person-times in the first quarter of 2018, ranking the first among Singapore's top 15 visitor-generating markets.

G Meanwhile, Chinese visitors spent about 1.05 billion Singapore dollars (about 0.77 billion U.S. dollars), excluding expenditure on Sightseeing, Entertainment & Gaming, in Singapore, 1 percent less than that for the same period of last year.

(307 words)

Notes

1. Alipay：支付宝由蚂蚁集团运营，是中国最大的移动支付平台，成立于2004年。
2. Singapore Tourism Board：新加坡旅游局是新加坡贸易和工业部下属的法定委员会。它支持新加坡重要经济支柱——旅游业的发展，并负责新加坡作为旅游目的地

的营销和推广。

Words

1. cashless   adj. 不用现金的
2. promote   v. 促进,推动;促销,推销;提升,晋升
3. various   adj. 各种不同的,各种各样的;具有多种特征的
4. demonstrate   vt. 证明,说明;表达,表现,显露;示范,演示
   vi. 示威
5. seamless   adj. 无缝的;(两部分之间)无空隙的,不停顿的
6. purchase   n. 购买,采购;购买的东西;握紧,抓牢
   vt. 买,购买,采购
   vi. 购买东西
7. accommodation   n. 住处,住宿;膳宿;和解,调解
8. partner   n. 配偶;合伙人,搭档;同伴,舞伴
   vi. 合伙,做搭档,配对
   vt. 使合伙
9. insight   n. 洞察力;领悟;洞悉,了解
10. explore   vi. 勘探,探索,考察,探究
    vt. 调查研究;探讨;勘查
11. compelling   adj. 引人入胜的;不可抗拒的;令人信服的
12. tailor   vt. 专门制作;为……做衣服
    vi. 做裁缝
    n. (尤指为顾客个别定制男装的)裁缝
13. merchant   n. 商人,批发商,(尤指)进出口批发商
    adj. 商人的;商船的
    vt. 经营,买卖
14. statistics   n. 统计数字;统计资料;统计学;(一项)统计数据
15. exclude   v. 不包括;不放在考虑之列;把……排斥在外
16. expenditure   n. 花费,消费;费用,开支

Useful Expressions

1. mobile payment 移动支付
2. cashless payment 无现金支付
3. provide...for... 提供;供应;给予

Difficult Sentences

1. According to a statement from Alipay, the trip was designed to promote Singapore's various destination offerings that accept Alipay's cashless payment platform to demonstrate to Chinese visitors that they can enjoy the same seamless experience in Singapore as they do back at home.

Chapter 5　Science and Technology　科学和技术

"that accept Alipay's cashless payment platform"是"destination offerings"的定语从句，" that they can enjoy the same seamless experience in Singapore as they do back at home."是动词不定式"to demonstrate"的宾语从句。

译文：根据支付宝的一份声明，此次旅行旨在推广新加坡的各种可以接受支付宝的无现金支付平台的度假胜地，让中国游客了解他们可以在新加坡无缝对接享受与国内一样的支付体验。

2. We are pleased to have partnered with Alipay in this activity given their strong reach and understanding of the Chinese market, our top source market for both visitor arrivals and tourist spending.

本句中 given 词性为介词，意思是考虑到，鉴于。

译文：我们很高兴与支付宝合作开展这项活动，因为他们对中国市场了解深入且影响巨大，而中国是我们游客和旅游消费的主要来源市场。

Reading Comprehension

There are five statements attached to the passage containing information given in one of the paragraphs. Identify the paragraph from which the information is derived and each paragraph is marked with a letter. You may only choose one paragraph once. Write down the letter in the blanks of each statement.

_____ 1. Alipay hopes to help more Singaporean businessmen to establish relationship with Chinese tourists.

_____ 2. Except expenses on sightseeing, entertainment and gaming, Chinese tourists spend vs ＄7.7 million less in Singapore than in the same period last year.

_____ 3. A cashless trip of Chinese tourists to Singapore for the first time was declared over on Thursday.

_____ 4. Because of the strong influence and understanding of the Chinese market, STB is very pleased to cooperate with Alipay.

_____ 5. One of the purposes of this trip is to show Chinese tourists that they can enjoy the same cashless experience in Singapore as in China.

Reading and Discussion

1. What's the agreement between Alipay and STB according to the news?
2. What's the purpose of this project from the perspective of SBT, according to Jacqueline Ng, director of the STB's Marketing Partnerships and Planning?
3. Why does SBT attach so much importance to the Chinese market?

Language in Use

Complete each sentence with a word listed below. Make changes where necessary.

purchase　compelling　demonstrate　cashless　statistics

1. The use of credit cards is making us a _____ society.

2. These results _____ convincingly that our campaign is working.
3. Official _____ show real wages declining by 24%.
4. The equipment can be _____ from your local supplier.
5. Her latest book makes _____ reading.

Chapter 6   Education

教育

ASEAN

前言

Reading 1

Economics teachers win awards for using apps to mark scripts and help students keep up with lessons
经济学教师因使用应用程序标记文本帮助学生学业进步而获奖

October 24, 2019 (*The Straits Times*)

A Hwa Chong Institution economics teacher Gilbert Ng, 39, noticed that second-year students in the junior college sometimes had to miss class if they were competing in inter-school tournaments during the sports season.

B To help them keep up with their studies, he worked with the National Institute of Education to create a "gamified flipped learning app" where students can access material such as quizzes and tutorial videos on their mobile phones. The app has been in use since 2017.

C Mr. Ng was one of two teachers who received the Outstanding Economics Teacher Award on Thursday (Oct 24) at the 12th Singapore Economic Policy Forum at the Regent Singapore hotel.

D The other recipient was Mr Koh Weining, 35, of Temasek Junior College, who has been actively involved in the piloting and refining of the MineGap app, which helps teachers mark scripts and give feedback more efficiently.

E Mr. Koh told The Straits Times that teachers sometimes get frustrated with pen-and-paper marking, having to write very similar comments while struggling with limited space to do so.

F The MineGap app, which Mr. Koh developed with Mr. Ng and another economics teacher, allows teachers to use a hashtag function from which they can retrieve saved comments, to customize it to students' needs. "Students have benefited from the more substantive feedback." said Mr. Koh, adding that the app was introduced last year.

G The award, given by the Economic Society of Singapore, recognizes teachers from secondary schools, junior college or centralized institutes who have contributed significantly towards the teaching and learning of economics in schools.

H Senior Minister of State for Trade and Industry Chee Hong Tat acknowledged the two teachers' achievements in his speech at the event on Thursday.

I He also revealed that while he did not study the subject earlier, he had taken on a second degree in economics at university and found it useful in understanding how economists think about issues and solve problems.

J He cited words from the late Professor Steve Goldman in his first economics class on how economics is not about money, but about understanding how incentives shape behaviors and influence outcomes.

K In his speech, Mr. Chee noted that economics alone cannot solve the challenges of the allocation and distribution of resources in society, amid a widening income gap and unequal distribution.

L　This is because countries will need to have the "right politics and also, set of social values which help to build broad-base support for these redistribution policies." But a good understanding of the subject can help design schemes to effectively redistribute resources, he told around 200 attendees at the forum.

(429 words)

>>> Notes

1. Hwa Chong Institution：华侨中学是新加坡首屈一指的私立学校，面向13岁至18岁的学生，涵盖中学及大学预科课程。

2. National Institute of Education：国立教育学院是新加坡南洋理工大学（Nanyang Technological University）的一个独立学院。

>>> Words

1. tournament　n. 锦标赛
2. tutorial　n.（大学导师的）个别辅导时间，辅导课
　　　　　adj. 导师的；私人教师的；辅导的
3. forum　n. 论坛，讨论会；（古罗马）公共集会场所
4. recipient　n. 受方接受者
　　　　　adj. 接受的
5. pilot　n. 飞行员；（飞行器）驾驶员；领航员
　　　　vt. 驾驶（飞行器）；领航（船只）；引导
　　　　adj. 试验性的，试点的
6. refine　vt. 精炼，提纯；去除杂质；改进，改善
　　　　vi. 被提炼
7. script　n. 剧本，电影剧本，广播（或讲话等）稿；手迹
　　　　vt. 为电影（或戏剧等）写剧本
　　　　vi. 写电影剧本
8. feedback　n. 反馈的意见（或信息）；（电器的）反馈噪音
　　　　　adj. 反馈的
9. frustrated　adj. 受挫的，失望的
10. hashtag　n. 推文话题（推特网上用带#号的词表示推文话题）
11. retrieve　v. 取回，索回；检索数据；扭转颓势；挽回，找回
　　　　　vi.（猎犬等）衔回猎物
　　　　　n. 衔回物
12. customize　vt. 订制，定做，改制（以满足顾主的需要）
13. substantive　adj. 实质性的，本质上的；重大的；严肃认真的
14. amid　prep. 在……过程中，在……中；随着
15. redistribution　n. 重新分配，重新分布
16. scheme　n. 计划，方案；体系，体制；阴谋，诡计，计谋

Chapter 6　Education 教育

　　　　　　　　vt. 密谋,秘密策划,图谋
　　　　　　　　vi. 搞阴谋;拟订计划

Useful Expressions

　　1. compete in 参加……比赛(竞赛)
　　2. keep up with 跟上,不落后
　　3. be involved in 包括,被卷入;涉及

Difficult Sentences

　　1. To help them keep up with their studies, he worked with the National Institute of Education to create a "gamified flipped learning app" where students can access material such as quizzes and tutorial videos on their mobile phones.

　　gamified flipped learning app 指游戏化翻转学习应用,句中 where 引导的定语从句,修饰先行词 gamified flipped learning app。

　　译文:为了帮助他们(学生)跟上学习进度,他与国立教育学院合作开发了一款"游戏化翻转学习应用程序",学生可以通过手机在这款应用程序上获取小测验和辅导视频等材料。

　　2. The MineGap app, which Mr. Koh developed with Mr. Ng and another economics teacher, allows teachers to use a hashtag function from which they can retrieve saved comments, to customize it to students' needs.

　　许先生与吴先生及另一位经济学教师共同开发的 MineGap 应用程序允许教师使用标签功能,从中检索保存的评语,并修改评语以满足学生的需要。

　　3. He cited words from the late Professor Steve Goldman in his first economics class on how economics is not about money, but about understanding how incentives shape behaviors and influence outcomes.

　　此句中"late"的意思是"已故的"。

　　译文:他引用了已故的史蒂夫戈德曼教授在他第一堂经济学课上的话。史蒂夫戈德曼教授谈到经济学不是关于金钱的科学,而是关于理解激励是如何塑造行为和影响结果的科学。

Reading Comprehension

　　There are five statements attached to the passage containing information given in one of the paragraphs. Identify the paragraph from which the information is derived and each paragraph is marked with a letter. You may only choose one paragraph once. Write down the letter in the blanks of each statement.

　　_____ 1. The MineGap app helps teachers to save comments according to students' needs to get more substantive feedback.

　　_____ 2. According to Mr. Koh, traditional written marking is frustrating.

　　_____ 3. The award is given to teachers who have made significant contributions to economic teaching in secondary schools, junior college or centralized institutes.

_____ 4. According to Chee Hong Tat, economics is very helpful to understand how economists thinking and solving problems.

_____ 5. Students can use this app to get materials such as tests and tutorial videos to keep up with their learning progress.

▶▶▶ Reading and Discussion

1. Why did Mr. Ng invent the MineGap app?
2. How does the MinGap app help students and teachers?
3. According to Chee Hong, the Senior Minister of State for Trade and Industry, how does economics help to solve the challenges of the allocation and distribution of resources?

▶▶▶ Language in Use

Complete each sentence with a word listed below. Make changes where necessary.

| refine   customize   redistribution   feedback   frustrated |

1. Wealth was _____ more equitably in society.
2. Oil is _____ to remove naturally occurring impurities.
3. I'd appreciate some _____ on my work.
4. You can _____ the software in several ways.
5. They felt _____ at the lack of progress.

Reading 2

UKM, RCSEd to promote rural surgery training
UKM, RCSEd 推进农村地区外科手术培训项目

October 30, 2019 (*New Straits Times*)

A The issue of having adequate housemanship placements for medical graduates could be addressed by encouraging them to take up postings in rural areas.

B The Royal College of Surgeons of Edinburgh (RCSEd), in collaboration with Universiti Kebangsaan Malaysia Medical Centre (UKMMC) and through the Tuanku Muhriz Travelling Fellowship, is looking at drafting up a program to train doctors in rural healthcare.

C RCSEd vice-president Dr. Pala Rajesh said the shortage of surgeons in Malaysia, a growing elderly population and trends towards increased healthcare utilization had contributed to a higher demand for the profession.

D "The country needs more surgeons and RCSEd wants to encourage junior doctors and medical students at their clinical years to pursue a career in surgery." he said.

E He said if RCSEd and UKMMC could get a model in place, they could share the programme with Asean countries that more or less faced the same challenges in rural healthcare.

Chapter 6　Education 教育

F　"Modern surgery is delivered in state-of-the-art infrastructure, with conditions that comply with a particular specialized surgeon's needs. But in rural areas, the surgeon needs a wider skill set that may not necessarily be comprehensive, but more generic in nature. That may be an attractive option for those thinking of embarking on a career in surgery." he said.

G　Dr Rajesh was speaking at the sidelines of the launch of RCSEd's International Strategy at UKMMC in Cheras, Kuala Lumpur.

H　The launch showcased the parties' commitment to deliver, promote and influence excellence and advancement in surgical practices and healthcare. It also aimed to promote the surgery as a career of choice among medical practitioners.

I　"RCSEd's role is not just developing the profession, but also to develop individuals. Surgical training is among the longest career pathways in medicine. Surgery is physically demanding in terms of daily routines in managing patients and performing practical procedures at all times of the day."

J　"To be a surgeon is not just about technical ability, but one needs to be technically excellent and pose good academic knowledge." said Dr Rajesh.

(353 words)

Notes

1. RCSEd(The Royal College of Surgeons of Edinburgh)：爱丁堡皇家外科医学院,是欧洲最古老的医学院之一,始建于公元1505年,距今已经有500余年历史。学院一直致力于外科医师的培训工作,为全世界输送了许多医学专业人才和医学大家,目前拥有会员超过28000人,分布在世界100多个国家中,是拥有巨大国际影响力的外科学专业机构。

2. UKMMC(Universiti Kebangsaan Malaysia Medical Centre)：马来西亚国立大学医疗中心。马来西亚国立大学是马来西亚几所研究性高校之一。马来西亚国立大学医疗中心隶属于马来西亚国立大学,位于蕉赖地区。

3. Cheras：蕉赖位于吉隆坡(Kuala Lumpur)的东南部,是吉隆坡人口最多的行政区。

Words

1. housemanship　n. (住院)实习医师的见习
2. address　n. 地址,所在地;演讲,致辞
　　　　　　vt. 写(收信人)姓名地址;设法解决;称呼;向……(作正式)讲话
　　　　　　vi. 准备;呼吁
3. collaboration　n. 合作,协作;合作成果(或作品)
4. draft　n. 草稿;草案;草图
　　　　　vt. 起草,草拟;选派,抽调
　　　　　vi. 起草
　　　　　adj. 初步画出或(写出)的;正在起草中的,草拟的

5. healthcare   n. 医疗保健,医疗卫生
6. utilization   n. 利用
7. clinical   adj. 临床的,临床诊断的;冷静的;朴素的
8. pursue   vt. 追求;追逐;追赶
            vi. 追赶;继续
9. surgery   n. 外科手术,外科学;门诊(时间)
10. surgeon   n. 外科医生
11. comply   vi. 遵从,服从,顺从
12. comprehensive   adj. 全部的,(几乎)无所不包的,综合的
                    n. 广告设计草样
13. generic   adj. 一般的,普通的,通用的;无商标的
                n. 通称
14. embark   vi. 上船;从事,着手
              vt. 使上船;使从事
15. showcase   n. 展示(本领、才华或优良品质)的场合;(商店或博物馆等的)玻璃柜台,玻璃陈列柜
                vt. 使展现;在玻璃橱窗内陈列
16. practitioner   n. (医学或法律界的)从业人员;从事者
17. pathway   n. 路径,途径
18. demanding   adj. 要求高的,需要高技能(或耐性等)的,费力的,苛求的,难满足的
19. procedure   n. (正常)程序,手续,步骤;常规

»»» Useful Expressions

1. take up 开始从事,开始干(工作)
2. demand for 对……的需求
3. advocate for 主张,提倡
4. in terms of 在……方面;从……角度看;根据……来说

»»» Difficult Sentences

1. The issue of having adequate housemanship placements for medical graduates could be addressed by encouraging them to take up postings in rural areas.
   address 在本句中的意思为"设法解决"。
   译文:通过鼓励医学毕业生到农村地区任职,可以为他们提供足够实习工作。

2. Modern surgery is delivered in state-of-the-art infrastructure, with conditions that comply with a particular specialized surgeon's needs. But in rural areas, the surgeon needs a wider skill set that may not necessarily be comprehensive, but more generic in nature.
   本句中 state-of-the-art 的意思是使用最先进技术的。
   译文:现代外科手术是在最先进的符合专业外科医生特定需要的基础设施中进行

的。但在农村地区，外科医生需要更广泛的技能，这些技能不一定是全面的，但实际上更通用。

Reading Comprehension

There are five statements attached to the passage containing information given in one of the paragraphs. Identify the paragraph from which the information is derived and each paragraph is marked with a letter. You may only choose one paragraph once. Write down the letter in the blanks of each statement.

_____ 1. RCSEd and UKMMC are willing to share the would-be model with other Asean countries in the future.

_____ 2. In rural areas, surgeons need a wider range of skills that are not necessarily comprehensive, but more generic.

_____ 3. Working in rural areas may help solve the problem of lacking adequate housemanship placements for medical graduates.

_____ 4. You need to have a good command of technique and academic knowledge to be a surgeon, according to Dr. Rajesh.

_____ 5. The International Strategy of RCSEd aims to encourage medical practitioners to take up surgery as their career of choice.

Reading and Discussion

1. Why are surgeons in high demand in Malaysia, according to Dr. Pala Rajesh?
2. What's the aim of RCSEd's International Strategy?
3. According to Dr. Rajesh what qualities do surgeons need?

Language in Use

Complete each sentence with a word listed below. Make changes where necessary.

address   collaboration   draft   pursue   demanding

1. This is only the first _____ of my speech.
2. Your essay does not _____ the real issues.
3. The work is physically _____.
4. She wrote the book in _____ with one of her students.
5. She wishes to _____ a medical career.

Reading 3

Top science high schools create innovative energy solutions in competition
顶级中学在竞争中找到创新的能源解决方案

May 8, 2018 (*The Philippine Star*)

A Shell, the Dutch global power, energy and gas giant, has announced the top science high schools that made it to the finals of the "The Bright Ideas Challenge Philippines" (TBIC), a national competition on innovative energy solutions that the company is introducing.

B "The competition isn't just a competition. It aims to spark students' curiosity in tackling real world problems through energy efficiency and other innovative ways." said Ramon del Rosario, vice president for external and government relations of Shell Companies in the Philippines (SciP), during the opening of the students' exhibit at the Mind Museum in BGC, Taguig.

C "We hope to inspire a generation of innovative Filipino scientists, thinkers, mentors, city planners and decision-makers through The Bright Ideas Challenge." he said.

D Out of 26 teams that submitted entries on how to sustainably power future cities, 10 chosen finalists were student groups from Meridian International Learning Experience, St. Theresa's College, CCF Life Academy, Dumaguete Science High School, Philippine Science High School Cagayan Valley, CEU Senior High School, and Biñan National High School.

E Sankie Simbulan, social performance and social investment manager of SCiP, said the competition aims to propel future leaders to think big and use teamwork and STEM in solving problems, particularly how future cities might run in cleaner and healthier ways.

F "We are also giving high school students a platform to be seen and heard, and help deliver the school curriculum through an innovative, more engaging approach." Simbulan said.

G Del Rosario added that the ideas of this year's finalists contain elements of sustainability, energy efficiency, science, technology and engineering.

H "The ideas here can be used in communities which don't have access to energy and water." he said.

I At the end of the competition, the student team from Philippine Science High School Cagayan Valley (Team Pisay CVC) and their prototype invention called "Pipe-to Manalo-to" was named grand prize winner. The team received a P100,000 prize package for their school that they can use to pursue their STEM program. In addition, the team also wins P100,000 and a fully-funded trip to attend the Make the Future festival in Singapore.

J ERMACC Energy Binan National High School was named first runner-up while second runner-up honors went to Centro Escolar University Senior High School. Also adjudged merit award winners were Team LIT Ideas and P for Power, both of Meridian Learning International Experience.

K The second prize winner received P70,000, plus another P70,000 for their school's STEM program, while the third prize winner received P50,000 plus another P50,000 prize package for their school's STEM program. The merit winners, meanwhile,

Chapter 6　Education 教育

each received a P10,000 prize package.

　　L　Team Pisay CVC of Philippine Science High School Cagayan Valley was able to miniaturize the principle of hydroelectric power generation for household application.

　　M　"Our idea can produce less than five kilowatts of electricity, which can charge a mobile phone and power house lights." said team leader John Paolo Lumanlan.

　　N　Lumanlan added that the generator uses a Kaplan propeller made from tin cans fitted into a pipe T-joint. The T-joint can replace the elbow joints of house water pipes and the water pressure runs the device like a dynamo with current flowing through an abutting electrical wire.

　　O　Designed to show how STEM can tackle real world problems, TBIC invited high school students from Grades 7 to 12, aged between 12 to 18 years old, to participate.

　　P　It is part of the Shell group's efforts to powering future cities and achieve its vision of a low carbon world.

　　(575 words)

Notes

1. Shell(Royal Dutch Shell Group):荷兰皇家壳牌石油公司成立于1833年,是世界上最大的石油公司之一,总部位于荷兰海牙。它由荷兰皇家石油和英国壳牌石油公司组成,是一个由能源和石化公司组成的全球集团,在世界70多个国家拥有80000多名员工。

2. STEM(Short for Science, Technology, Engineering and Math):STEM是科学、技术、工程和数学的简称,它是培养年轻人创造性解决问题的能力的一种跨学科的方法。

3. Kaplan propeller:1913年,奥地利的卡普兰教授发明了螺旋桨式水轮机,是在弗朗西斯水轮机基础上发展而来的。这种水轮机被称为卡普兰螺旋桨式水轮机。

Words

1. energy　n. 精力,活力,力量;能源
2. spark　n. 火花,火星;电火花;微量,一点儿
　　　　vi. 冒火花,飞火星,产生电火花
　　　　vt. 引发,触发,激励
3. curiosity　n. 好奇心,求知欲;罕见而有趣之物
4. tackle　vt. 应付,处理,解决(难题或局面)
　　　　n. 用具,装备
　　　　vi. (足)阻截
5. efficiency　n. 效率,效能,功效
6. external　adj. 外部的,外面的;外界的;在外的
　　　　　n. 外部,外面;外观;外部情况
7. submit　vt. 使屈服,顺从,屈服,投降
　　　　vi. 提交,呈递(文件、建议等)

8. sustainably   adv. 可持续地
9. sustainability   n. 耐久性
10. propel   vt. 推动,驱动,推进
11. prototype   n. 原型;典型
12. merit   n. 优点,价值;值得赞扬(或奖励、钦佩)的特点;功绩
              vt. 应得;值得
              vi. 应受报答
13. miniaturize   v. 使微型化
14. principle   n. 道德原则,行为准则;原则,原理
15. hydroelectric   adj. 使用水力发电的;水力产生的
16. kilowatt   n. 千瓦(电的功率计量单位,等于1000瓦特)
17. dynamo   n. 发电机;精力充沛的人
18. abut   vi. 邻接,毗连,紧靠
            vt. 与……邻接
19. carbon   n. 碳;复写纸

Useful Expressions

1. aim to do 旨在做某事
2. energy efficiency 能效
3. have access to 使用;接近;可以利用

Difficult Sentences

1. Shell, the Dutch global power, energy and gas giant, has announced the top science high schools that made it to the finals of the "The Bright Ideas Challenge Philippines" (TBIC), a national competition on innovative energy solutions that the company is introducing.

本句中第一个 that 引导的定语从句修饰先行词 schools,该定语从句中还包含另一个由 that 引导的定语从句,修饰先行词 solutions。

译文:荷兰的全球电力、能源和天然气巨头——壳牌公司宣布进入了"菲律宾绝妙创意挑战"决赛的顶尖科学中学名单,该赛事是由壳牌公司推行的全国性创新能源解决方案竞赛。

2. Lumanlan added that the generator uses a Kaplan propeller made from tin cans fitted into a pipe T-joint. The T-joint can replace the elbow joints of house water pipes and the water pressure runs the device like a dynamo with current flowing through an abutting electrical wire.

本句中 made from tin cans 是过去分词短语作名词,为 propeller 的后置定语,可以改成定语从句 which is made from tin cans。

译文:卢曼兰补充说,发电机使用的是一个由锡罐做成的卡普兰螺旋桨,装在T形管接头上。该T形接头可代替家用水管的肘形接头,水压使装置像发电机一样运转,电流就会流过连接的电线。

Chapter 6　Education 教育

》》》Reading Comprehension

There are five statements attached to the passage containing information given in one of the paragraphs. Identify the paragraph from which the information is derived and each paragraph is marked with a letter. You may only choose one paragraph once. Write down the letter in the blanks of each statement.

_____ 1. Students aged between 12 to 18 years old are invited to take part in the competition.

_____ 2. According to Del Rosario the ideas of this year's finalists can be applied to communities lacking energy and water.

_____ 3. A handmade Kaplan propeller is used in a generator made by Team Pisay CVC.

_____ 4. According to Ramon del Rosario the competition is expected to stimulate students' curiosity through solving real world problems.

_____ 5. The purpose of this competition is to promote high school students to solve problems with team spirit and STEM according to Sankie Simbulan.

》》》Reading and Discussion

1. Why does Shell introduce The Bright Ideas Challenge (TBIC) to the Philippines, according to Ramon del Rosario?

2. How many teams submitted entries on how to sustainably power future cities?

3. Which team won the grand prize?

》》》Language in Use

Complete each sentence with a word listed below. Make changes where necessary.

spark　curiosity　tackle　external　principle

1. Stick to your _____ and tell him you won't do it.

2. The government is determined to _____ inflation.

3. Children show _____ about everything.

4. A combination of internal and _____ factors caused the company to close down.

5. The proposal would _____ a storm of protest around the country.

Chapter 7 Culture

文化

ASEAN

文化

Reading 1

Singaporean PM Encourages More Efforts to Use Mandarin
新加坡总理鼓励更多努力使用普通话

October 23, 2019 (*China Daily*)

A Singaporean Prime Minister Lee Hsien Loong on Tuesday encouraged citizens to make more efforts to use and improve their Mandarin.

B The prime minister made the call at an event marking the 40th anniversary of the Speak Mandarin Campaign at the Singapore Chinese Cultural Centre.

C "People all over the world are learning Mandarin eagerly. They all know that to work in China, to build relationships with the Chinese, and to grab opportunities that come with China's development, they have to master Mandarin." he said.

D The Speak Mandarin Campaign was first launched in 1979 to encourage Singaporeans to speak Mandarin.

E Mandarin has helped unify Singapore's Chinese community, strengthening kinship and enabling a deeper understanding of Singapore's Chinese culture. Moving forward, the Speak Mandarin Campaign aims to help Singaporeans build the capability and confidence to use Mandarin effectively in different contexts, as it continues to create conducive environments for Mandarin to be used and practiced.

F "We have to put in more effort to encourage the use of Mandarin in our daily lives, and find ways to keep the language alive and preserve the uniqueness of our Mandarin." said the prime minister.

G While most young Chinese Singaporeans today can understand and speak Mandarin, they may not speak it fluently, he noted.

H The Mandarin that Singaporeans speak and use carries unique nuances in vocabulary and turns of phrase. Singaporeans can soon find these Singaporean Mandarin terms in a newly created online Singaporean Mandarin database. The database features commonly used and unique Singaporean terms which reflect and celebrate Singapore's multi-ethnic heritage and identity, according to experts.

I Led by Principal Investigator and Promote Mandarin Council member Tan Chee Lay, the research project aims to compile the Singaporean Mandarin database over two years, and will include terms that Singaporeans would have ascribed cultural, historical or sentimental value to. These terms are used in Singapore but may not be commonly used in other Mandarin speaking regions.

J The Promote Mandarin Council has collaborated with Business China to identify and recognize eight young bilingual professionals, whose language capability in Mandarin has helped them in their professional careers, or enriched their personal lives.

K "This is a milestone year for the Speak Mandarin Campaign and we are encouraged that many believe Mandarin to be integral to strengthening a unique Singaporean Chinese identity. With this year's initiatives, we encourage everyone to embody the right attitudes, and to play active roles to encourage the use of Mandarin." Chua Chim Kang, chairman of the Promote Mandarin Council, said.

(412 words)

Notes

1. Lee Hsien Loong:新加坡总理李显龙。1952年2月10日出生于新加坡,毕业于哈佛大学,现任新加坡第三任总理,新加坡人民行动党秘书长。
2. Speak Mandarin Campaign:"讲华语运动"是新加坡建国总理李光耀先生在1979年发起的,目的是要鼓励新加坡华人"多讲华语,少说方言",提高华语的水平。
3. Promote Mandarin Council:推广华语理事会,负责讲华语运动。

Words

1. mandarin　n. 普通话,官话,国语
　　　　　　adj. 官僚的
2. launch　vt. 使(船)下水;使……开始运作;首创
　　　　　vi. 开始;积极投入
3. unify　v. 联合;统一;成一体
4. kinship　n. 血缘关系,亲属关系;(性质等)类似
5. unique　adj. 独一无二的;独特的;罕有的;极不寻常的
　　　　　n. 独一无二的人
6. nuance　n.(意义、感情、颜色、音调等的)细微差别
　　　　　vt. 精确细腻地表达
7. heritage　n. 继承财产,遗产;继承物
8. identity　n. 身份,本体;同一性,一致
9. identify　vt. 指认;认为……等同于;使参与
　　　　　vi. 成为一体;认同
10. compile　vt. 汇编;编辑;编纂;编译
11. ascribe　vt. 把……归因于;把……归属(于)
12. collaborate　vi. 合作,协作
13. bilingual　adj. 流利地讲两种语言的;双语的;能用同一种语言的两种形式的;使用两种语言的
　　　　　　n. 熟谙两种语言的人
14. integral　adj. 必需的,必要的;基本的,基础的;完整的
　　　　　　n. 积分;整数
15. initiative　n. 首创精神;创造力;主动性;积极性

Useful Expressions

1. keep the language alive 保持语言鲜活
2. preserve the uniqueness 保持独特性
3. embody the right attitudes 拥有正确的态度
4. the Singaporean Mandarin database 新加坡华语资料库

Chapter 7　Culture 文化

Difficult Sentences

1. "People all over the world are learning Mandarin eagerly. They all know that to work in China, to build relationships with the Chinese, and to grab opportunities that come with China's development, they have to master Mandarin." he said.

　　本句中的 they all know that 中的 that 是宾语从句的引导词,引导宾语从句 that they have to master Mandarin,意思为他们都知道他们必须掌握普通话。三个并列的不定式短语 to work in China;to build relationships with the Chinese;to grab opportunities that come with China's development 是目的性状语,其中 to grab opportunities that come with China's development 中的 that come with China's development 是定语从句,修饰 opportunities。意思是在中国工作,与中国人建立关系,抓住中国发展带来的机遇。

　　译文:他说:"世界各地的人正在积极学习普通话。他们都知道,如果要在中国工作、与中国人打交道、把握住中国发展所带来的商机,他们就必须学好普通话。"

2. Moving forward, the Speak Mandarin Campaign aims to help Singaporeans build the capability and confidence to use Mandarin effectively in different contexts, as it continues to create conducive environments for Mandarin to be used and practiced.

　　本句 as it continues ... practiced 中 as 引导的是方式状语从句,意思为正如它持续创造有助于普通话的使用和实践的环境。different contexts:不同的环境。

　　译文:进一步说,"讲华语运动"的目标是帮助新加坡人建立在不同情况下有效使用普通话的能力和信心,正如它持续为使用和练习普通话创造有利的环境。

Reading Comprehension

There are five statements attached to the passage containing information given in one of the paragraphs. Identify the paragraph from which the information is derived and each paragraph is marked with a letter. You may only choose one paragraph once. Write down the letter in the blanks of each statement.

　　_____ 1. The Prime Minister mentioned that most young Chinese Singaporeans may not speak fluent Mandarin even though they can understand and speak it.

　　_____ 2. It was in 1979 that the Speak Mandarin Campaign was carried out in order to prompt Singaporeans to speak Mandarin.

　　_____ 3. Some terms are only spoken by Singaporeans.

　　_____ 4. This year is a landmark for the Speak Mandarin Campaign. Many Singaporeans believe that Mandarin plays an essential role for enhancing a distinctive Singaporean Chinese identity.

　　_____ 5. An online Singaporean Mandarin database which is newly founded can provide Singaporeans with Singaporean Mandarin terms.

Reading and Discussion

　　1. What's the purpose of the Speak Mandarin Campaign launched in Singapore in

1979?

2. In what way can Mandarin benefit Singaporean?

3. What's the uniqueness of Singaporean Mandarin terms complied in online Singaporean Mandarin database?

Language in Use

Complete each sentence with a word listed below. Make changes where necessary.

launch   unify   ascribe   kinship   bilingual

1. Children who grow up in _____ households have a distinct advantage over their peers.

2. We _____ a big advertising campaign to promote our new toothpaste last month.

3. The world always seems to _____ financial success to superior intelligence.

4. He pledged to _____ the city's political factions.

5. The ties of _____ may have helped the young man find his way in life.

Reading 2

Vietnam's Booming Craft Beer Scene
越南蓬勃发展的精酿啤酒业

September 7, 2017 (CNN)

A A night out drinking in Vietnam used to mean one thing: sipping Bia Hoi, a local draft beer with 3% alcohol content, from a tiny stool on the sidewalk.

B But feather-light lagers aren't the only game in town anymore. The country's craft beer scene is booming, having welcomed more than a dozen micro-breweries in the past two years.

C "The beer culture in Vietnam starts with Bia Hoi." Hao Tran, managing editor of lifestyle website *Vietcetera*, tells CNN. The craft beer scene that has evolved has done so from people drinking beer in the Old Quarter in Hanoi or Bui Vien Street in Saigon, he says, "But there's so much more to beer culture in Vietnam now than just that particular image."

Tapping new tastes

D Vietnam is one of the biggest beer consumers in Asia drinking 3.8 billion liters a year in 2016, according to Ministry of Industry and Trade.

E While stalwart brands such as Tiger, Saigon Beer, and Bia Hoi still account for the lion's share of that consumption, in Ho Chi Minh City alone artisan brewers such as Platinum, Pasteur Street Brewing Co, Winking Seal, Heart of Darkness, and Fuzzy Logic are providing a real alternative, says Tran.

F The brands have, for example, introduced potent Indian pale ales (IPAs) and sour gose — a tart and salty style of German beer — to the market.

G "As Vietnam has continued to experience income growth and taste for global concepts and standards, that's where craft beer has really come in," says Tran, "The tastes and preferences of Vietnamese consumers are changing and evolving."

A welcome change

H While many of the first microbreweries were set up by foreigners, Vietnamese entrepreneurs have also joined the mix.

I Newly opened *East West Brewing Company*, for example, is run by Loc Truong, a Vietnamese-American who worked at Anheuser-Busch InBev — the company behind brands such as Stella Artois and Corona — before striking out with his founding partners.

J "My being Vietnamese helps the craft beer industry, for sure, because that's one step to connect with the market," says Truong, who was born in Vietnam but studied in the US. "Why do people buy craft beer? It's higher quality, but who's behind it also adds value."

K Truong's lightly hopped beers, such as the East West Pale Ale, he says, provide a stepping stone to stronger flavors for new craft converts.

L From there, it gets more challenging, with a bolder Far East IPA, Coffee Vanilla Porter, or 12% ABV Independence Stout.

M That's alongside Asia-inspired varieties, such as Le Wit, a wit-style beer made with Asian pear, and a dainty Saigon Rose that's infused with raspberries.

N "A lot of people don't know that there are so many different types of flavors in beer." says Truong.

O "We'll see customers coming back five or six times a week, saying they can't drink the traditional lagers or (Bia Hoi beer) anymore. Once they tried craft, they never went back."

(485 words)

Notes

1. Bia Hoi:越南鲜啤酒,这是一种快速发酵的啤酒,酒精度一般不超过3%,据说是世界上最便宜的生啤酒。
2. Hanoi:越南首都河内市,有"千年文物之地"的美称。著名景点有巴亭广场、主席府、还剑湖等。
3. Bui Vien Street:胡志明市著名的"背包客一条街"——碧文街,里面有很多物美价廉的旅店。
4. Saigon:西贡,越南城市胡志明市的旧称。1975年4月30日,越南战争结束后,为纪念越南共产党的主要创立者胡志明,便将西贡改名为"胡志明市"。
5. Ho Chi Minh City:越南胡志明市,也称西贡,为越南最大的城市。
6. Indian pale ales (IPAs):印度淡色艾尔,一种淡麦芽酒的统称,制作时使用了颜色更淡的烤麦芽。

>>> Words

1. boom　n. 迅速增长；繁荣；低沉有回响的声音
　　　　vi. 繁荣迅速发展；发出隆隆声
　　　　vt. 使繁荣
　　　　adj. 发展中的
2. sip　vi. 小口地喝
　　　vt. 呷；抿
　　　n. 一小口之量；一啜或一呷之量
3. lager　n. 窖藏啤酒；贮陈啤酒
4. micro-brewery　n.（使用传统方法酿造啤酒的）微型啤酒厂，小酿酒厂
5. evolve　vt. 使逐步形成；释放；引申出
　　　　vi. 演化；进化
6. stalwart　adj. 健壮的，强壮的；勇敢的；坚定的
　　　　　n. 坚定的支持者，坚定分子；健壮的人
7. alternative　adj. 两者（或两者以上）择一的；供选择的
　　　　　　n. 两者（或在两者以上之间）择一；供选择的东西
8. potent　adj. 强势的，强有力的；影响巨大的；（药等）功效强的
9. dainty　adj. 精致的；优雅的；可口的，美味的
　　　　n. 美食；佳肴
10. infuse　vt.（向……）灌输；使充满
　　　　vi.（茶叶、药草等）被浸

>>> Useful Expressions

1. local draft beer 本地生啤酒
2. craft beer 精酿啤酒
3. income growth 收入增长
4. global concepts and standards 全球概念和标准

>>> Difficult Sentences

1. "As Vietnam has continued to experience income growth and taste for global concepts and standards, that's where craft beer has really come in," says Tran, "The tastes and preferences of Vietnamese consumers are changing and evolving."

本句 As Vietnam has continued to experience income growth and taste for global concepts and standards 是由 as 引导原因状语从句，表示"由于，因为"。主句是 that's where craft beer has really come in 表示这就是精酿啤酒发展起来的诱因。

译文："随着越南当地人收入的持续增长和体验到全球的概念和标准，精酿啤酒才真正有了市场，"Tran 说，"越南消费者的口味和偏好正在改变和提升。"

2. "My being Vietnamese helps the craft beer industry, for sure, because that's one step to connect with the market," says Truong, who was born in Vietnam but studied in the US.

本句中,for sure 是插入语,because that's one step to connect with the market 是原因状语从句,who 引导的定语从句修饰 Truong。

译文:"我的越南人身份当然有助于精酿啤酒行业与市场建立更进一步的联系。"出生在越南但在美国求学的 Truong 说。

Reading Comprehension

There are five statements attached to the passage containing information given in one of the paragraphs. Identify the paragraph from which the information is derived and each paragraph is marked with a letter. You may only choose one paragraph once. Write down the letter in the blanks of each statement.

_____ 1. The statistics of Ministry of Industry and Trade shows that as a one of the biggest beer consumers in Asia, in 2016, Vietnamese drank 3800 million liters beer.

_____ 2. According to Truong, many people don't know that beer has multiple flavors.

_____ 3. Many small-sized breweries have been set up in the past two years because of the prosperity of craft beer scene in Vietnam.

_____ 4. Vietnam's beer culture began with Bia Hoi.

_____ 5. Drinking Bia Hoi from a very small stool on the sidewalk used to be the only way for night out drinking in Vietnam.

Reading and Discussion

1. Who set up many of the first microbreweries in Vietnam?
2. What led to the prosperity of craft beer scene in Vietnam?
3. What does the sentence "Once they tried craft, they never went back." imply?

Language in Use

Complete each sentence with a word listed below. Make changes where necessary.

boom   evolve   alternative   infuse   potent

1. In addition, the corporation may lose the opportunity to _____ flexibility into the IT portfolio.

2. By 1988 the economy was _____.

3. He said there is no _____ for him but to maintain order under any circumstances.

4. Nature photography has become a _____ tool in this struggle.

5. All of this is done by using techniques and technologies that have been around for years but which have continued to _____.

Poor, Rural Students in Laos Lack Tech to Learn From Home
老挝贫穷的农村学生缺乏在家里学习的技术设备

April 8, 2020 (VOA)

A COVID-19 has forced Laos to join countries around the world in closing schools and using online distance learning. But rural and urban poor students in Laos not only lack computers and access to the internet —some even live in homes without electricity.

B The ninth poorest of the 10 members of the ASEAN in terms of GDP, Laos' underfunded education system has been struggling since long before the coronavirus started spreading in the region.

C Families with students in the town of Vang Vieng, Vientiane province, told RFA that the students in their households lacked access to smartphones or computers while they are being told to study at home. "The students stopped learning since schools closed down. They can't use YouTube to learn because our village doesn't even have electricity." one Vang Vieng mother told RFA Wednesday. But despite not being connected to the grid, she said the family is making the best of the situation. "They will just keep doing their homework assigned by their teachers before the closure. We parents must help them to do their homework." she said.

D Teachers were caught off guard by the government's announcement that schools were closing, so they hastily made homework assignments without knowing how long the schools would be closed.

E Students in the more affluent and well-connected cities are at an advantage over their rural peers. "About 80 percent of students are learning on smartphones or computers at home. The teachers are conducting lessons on WhatsApp," the father of a student at a private international school in the Lao capital city Vientiane told RFA. But even in the cities, there is a disparity between rich and poor, and the latter's limited access to tech is making distance education difficult. "The rest of the students are not able to learn online because they don't have those devices." the father said.

F A teacher at the international school explained how those who have no access to tech have been faring, saying, "Parents who have smartphones and computers can forward homework to their children. They can do their homework, which the parents can then send back to the teachers." "If the teachers find any mistakes, they verbally correct them on the app telling students the answers are incorrect. This is how we do it." said the teacher. The teacher added that all the teachers had advised the students and their parents that they have to do their homework and send it back or else they would not receive marks and would lag behind.

G Students that have been distance learning have complained that it is ineffective. "Learning online is more difficult than learning in the classroom or in front of a professor. It's a lot harder to understand." a student at the National University of Laos told RFA.

"We don't have video conference calls. The professor only posts video clips on WhatsApp and then the students can learn from home." the student said.

(486 words)

Notes

1. Vang Vieng：老挝的城市万荣，位于万象省北部，以喀斯特地貌和山间湖边的户外活动闻名。

2. Vientiane：老挝的首都万象。万象市沿湄公河延伸，呈新月形，故有月亮城之说。市内多寺庙、古塔，其建筑有热带风格和老挝艺术的特点。

Words

1. underfunded   adj.（机构、项目）缺乏资金的，资金不足的
2. coronavirus   n. 冠状病毒
3. grid   n. 网格；格子，栅格；输电网
           vt. 将……布成网格状的
           adj. [美口]橄榄球的
4. assign   vt. 分配；指派
            vi. 将财产过户（尤指过户给债权人）
            n. 受让人
5. closure   n. 关闭；结束
             vt. 以提付表决来终止（某人）发言
             vi. 采用终止辩论提付表决的办法
6. hastily   adv. 匆忙地，急速地，慌忙地
7. disparity   n. 不同，不一致，不等
8. verbally   adv. 口头地，非书面地；用言辞地
9. complain   vi. 投诉，发牢骚；控告
              vt. 抱怨；控诉

Useful Expressions

1. online distance learning 在线远程学习
2. access to the internet 接入互联网
3. catch off guard 猝不及防

Difficult Sentences

1. Families with students in the town of Vang Vieng, Vientiane province, told RFA that the students in their households lacked access to smartphones or computers while they are being told to study at home.

本句中，with 引导的介词短语作定语修饰 families，主干部分为 families told RFA。that 引导的是宾语从句，while 引导的是时间状语从句。

译文：在万象省的万荣市，有学生的家庭告诉 RFA，他们家里的学生在被告知要在家学习时没有智能手机或电脑。

2. Teachers were caught off guard by the government's announcement that schools were closing, so they hastily made homework assignments without knowing how long the schools would be closed.

本句中,that schools were closing 是同位语从句说明 announcement 的内容,so 引导的是原因状语从句。

译文:政府宣布将关闭学校,这让老师们措手不及,所以他们匆忙地布置家庭作业,却不知道学校将关闭多长时间。

3. A teacher at the international school explained how those who have no access to tech have been faring, saying, "Parents who have smartphones and computers can forward homework to their children. They can do their homework, which the parents can then send back to the teachers."

本句中,explain 后接 how 引导的从句作宾语,who 引导的定语从句修饰 those。

译文:这所国际学校的一名老师解释了那些无法接触到科技产品的学生是如何做作业的,他说:"有智能手机和电脑的父母可以把作业给他们的孩子看。孩子做完作业后,家长再把作业发给老师。"

Reading Comprehension

There are five statements attached to the passage containing information given in one of the paragraphs. Identify the paragraph from which the information is derived and each paragraph is marked with a letter. You may only choose one paragraph once. Write down the letter in the blanks of each statement.

_____ 1. Students are told to learn at home due to the closure of schools. However, students from rural and urban poor families in Laos lack tech to learn online.

_____ 2. Like many countries around the world, Laos has to close schools and Launch the distance learning activities on the net because of COVID-19.

_____ 3. The effect of learning online is not as efficient as the learning in the classroom.

_____ 4. 80% of students in more prosperous city with good internet connection are learning online via WhatsApp.

_____ 5. All the teachers suggest that students and their parents must do their homework and send it back.

Reading and Discussion

1. Why does Laos close schools and use online distant learning?
2. What did the teachers do after being caught off guard by the government's announcement?
3. What are the difficulties that students in Laos faced when learning online and what the complaint of the students that have been distant learning?

Chapter 7 Culture 文化

》》 Language in Use

Complete each sentence with a word listed below. Make changes where necessary.

underfunded   assign   access   disparity   complain

1. When I taught, I would _____ a topic to children that they would write about.

2. Physiological _____ are quite striking among races.

3. But schools themselves remain _____ and the quality of education remains poor.

4. Miners have _____ bitterly that the government did not fulfill their promises.

5. For logistical and political reasons, scientists have only recently been able to gain _____ to the area.

Chapter 8 Environment

环境

ASEAN

Reading 1
Bacteria and Fungi Show a Precise Daily Rhythm in Tropical Air
热带空气中细菌与真菌呈现精确的每日节奏

October 30, 2019 (*Science Daily*)

A Scientists from the Singapore Centre for Environmental Life Sciences Engineering (SCELSE) at Nanyang Technological University, Singapore (NTU Singapore) have found that the air in the tropics is teeming with a rich and diverse range of at least 725 different microorganisms.

B The NTU scientists used a new sampling and DNA sequencing protocol of microbial communities in Singapore's air. They found that the composition of the microbial community in the tropical air changes predictably, with bacteria dominating in the day and fungi at night.

C In the research paper led by NTU genomics professor Stephan Schuster, the team reported that tropical air had a microbial diversity with similar complexity to other well-studied ecosystems, such as seawater, soil, and the human gut.

D These bioaerosol communities (airborne particles of biological origin) have an unexpectedly high number of bacterial and fungal species, and they follow a diel cycle (a 24-hour day and night cycle) which scientists believe is driven by environmental conditions such as humidity, rain, solar irradiance and carbon dioxide levels.

E They also demonstrate a greater variation in composition within a day than between days or even months. This robust community structure maintains long-term predictability, despite variations in airflow and monsoonal winds across the tropical seasons.

F Professor Schuster, who is a research director at SCELSE, said having the ability to analyse bioaerosols provides insights into many aspects of urban life that affect our daily living and human well-being. It also provides an understanding of the interactions between atmospheric, terrestrial and aquatic planetary ecosystems, which is particularly valuable during climate change.

G The scientists say they are beginning to understand the effect of air microbial communities on the environment and human health, with the most immediate impact on patients with respiratory illnesses. Further, damage to agricultural crops could be avoided long term, as many of the detected organisms are plant pathogens or wood rotting fungi.

H Previous studies by other research groups have reported bioaerosol communities based on either cultivation or gene amplification, both of which incur substantial biases and aggregates of time, without however achieving a temporal resolution that would have allowed for observing the daily cycling of airborne microorganisms.

I Team member Dr. Elena Gusareva, a postdoctoral research fellow at NTU said the unprecedented scale and depth of analysis and classification, allowed the team to identify more than 1,200 bacterial and fungal species that perform a changing pattern of microbial community composition.

　　J　Ongoing research at NTU is now looking at using the same method to analyse bioaerosols globally at other sites, which could yield similar trends in terms of following the diel cycle.

　　(425 words)

⟫⟫ Notes

　　1. Centre for Environmental Life Sciences Engineering：环境生命科学工程中心。南洋理工大学的国家级环境与生命研究基地。

　　2. Nanyang Technological University：南洋理工大学。简称南大(NTU)，是新加坡的一所世界著名的研究型大学。

⟫⟫ Words

　　1. bacteria　n.(复数)细菌
　　2. fungi　n.(fungus 的复数)菌类；蘑菇；霉菌
　　3. microorganism　n. 微生物
　　4. protocol　n. 外交礼仪；草案；协议；规章制度；科学实验报告
　　　　　　　　vi. 拟定(或颁布)议定书
　　　　　　　　vt. 把……写入议定书
　　5. microbial　adj. 微生物的；由细菌引起的
　　6. genomics　n. [复](用作单)基因组学
　　7. bioaerosol　n. 生物气溶胶
　　8. fungal　adj. 真菌的，由真菌引起的；短暂的(＝fungous)
　　　　　　　n. 真菌类植物(＝fungus)
　　9. diel　adj. 一昼夜的
　　　　　　n. 一昼夜
　　10. irradiance　n. 发光，光辉；[物]辐照度
　　11. monsoonal　adj. 季风的
　　12. respiratory　adj. 呼吸的；与呼吸有关的
　　13. pathogen　n. 病原体
　　14. aggregate　adj. 合计的，总的；聚集的
　　　　　　　　n. 总计；集成体
　　　　　　　　vt. (使)聚集；总计
　　　　　　　　vi. 聚集
　　15. temporal　adj. 现世的；暂存的；时态的

⟫⟫ Useful Expressions

　　1. microbial communities 微生物群落
　　2. aquatic planetary ecosystems 水生行星生态系统

Chapter 8　Environment 环境

Difficult Sentences

1. In the research paper led by NTU genomics professor Stephan Schuster, the team reported that tropical air had a microbial diversity with similar complexity to other well-studied ecosystems, such as seawater, soil, and the human gut.

本句带了一个 with 的并列结构，作为 a microbial diversity 的协同成分。

译文：在南洋理工大学基因组学教授斯蒂芬·舒斯特所主持的研究报告中，研究小组指出热带空气有着微生物的多样性，并且具备与其他已充分研究过的生态系统相似的复杂性，如海水、土壤和人类肠道系统等。

2. Professor Schuster, who is a research director at SCELSE, said having the ability to analyse bioaerosols provides insights into many aspects of urban life that affect our daily living and human well-being.

本句中"having the ability to analyse bioaerosols"是由动名词所构成的宾语从句的主语，"that affect our daily living and human well-being"是定语从句，修辞 many aspects of urban life。

译文：环境生命科学工程中心的研究主任舒斯特教授说道，拥有分析生物气溶胶的能力可以让我们了解影响人们每天生活与人类健康的城市生活的许多方面。

3. Previous studies by other research groups have reported bioaerosol communities based on either cultivation or gene amplification, both of which incur substantial biases and aggregates of time, without however achieving a temporal resolution that would have allowed for observing the daily cycling of airborne microorganisms.

本句用 both of which 引导了一个表示所有格的定语从句"both of which incur substantial biases and aggregates of time"来修辞 cultivation 和 gene amplification。

译文：由其他研究机构进行的前期研究表明由培养或基因扩充而形成的生物气溶胶共生体，均会导致大量轮次的偏差与集合，从而无法获取观察空气微生物每日循环的暂时性解决方案。

Reading Comprehension

There are five statements attached to the passage containing information given in one of the paragraphs. Identify the paragraph from which the information is derived and each paragraph is marked with a letter. You may only choose one paragraph once. Write down the letter in the blanks of each statement.

_____ 1. The air microbial communities have the most immediate impact on patients with respiratory diseases.

_____ 2. The NTU scientists conducted research on Singapore's air and found out the composition of the microbial community with a new sampling and DNA sequencing protocol.

_____ 3. A diel cycle in 24-hour cycle is followed by the bioaerosol communities with a high number of bacterial and fungal species.

_____ 4. More experiments are expected to be carried on in other countries with the same method to analyse bioaerosols.

_____ 5. The variation in composition in a day is much bigger than that between days or even months.

Reading and Discussion

1. What is the microbial diversity in tropical air similar to?
2. What can the ability to analyse bioaerosols endow us?
3. What can't the previous studies in bioaerosol communities achieve?

Language in Use

Complete each sentence with a word listed below. Make changes where necessary.

bacteria microorganism respiratory aggregate temporal

1. The patients suffering from _____ disease will be affected by the air microbial communities.

2. _____ hold a vast diversity in the tropical air.

3. In the tropical areas, _____ and fungi in the air cause great interests in scientific researches.

4. A _____ solution to deal with the air microbial communities is far from enough.

5. The substantial biases and _____ of time will result from either cultivation or gene amplification.

Reading 2

Better Protection Sought for Thailand's Helmeted Hornbill
泰国寻求更好保护盔犀鸟的方法

October 11, 2019 (*The Associated Press News*)

A   BANGKOK — Time is running out for Thailand's dwindling population of helmeted hornbills thanks to poaching of the exotic birds for the ivory-like casques atop their big red and yellow beaks.

B   The species, known by the scientific name Rhinoplax vigil, is listed as "critically endangered" by the International Union for Conservation of Nature. "Currently, there are fewer than 100 of the birds in Thailand's forests." says Dr. Kaset Sutacha, chairman of the Bird Conservation Society of Thailand and head of the Exotic Pet and Wildlife Clinic at Kasetsart University's Faculty of Veterinary Medicine in Bangkok.

C   "Critically endangered" is just a step away from "extinct in the wild" and two steps from becoming considered "extinct".

D   Demand from China is helping drive demand for their distinctive casques, "helmets" in French, which males deploy in battle. The material is used to make rings, pendants and other decorative items.

E Worries over the species' survival intensified after the wildlife trade monitoring group TRAFFIC recently posted photos online of dozens of skulls of the endangered avian for sale.

F A campaign on the change. org online petition site is pressuring the government to add the bird to Thailand's Wildlife Preservation List as soon as possible. It now lists 19 other species.

G The bird is already on Thailand's official list of protected animals, but would get much better protection if it's included in the Wildlife Preservation List, Kaset said. That "means we can get money, officers and tools from the government, including a national conservation plan designed just for this species." he said.

H The population of the bird, found in Indonesia, Malaysia and parts of Myanmar and southern Thailand, is dwindling, the IUCN says. Most types of hornbills have hollow casques. The helmeted hornbills' are a hard, solid block that in the illegal wildlife market is called "red ivory".

I The London-based Environmental Investigation Agency says black market prices are up to five times higher than for elephant tusks. China appears to be the main market for helmeted hornbill parts and products, though there is also demand in Laos and Thailand, says Elizabeth John, TRAFFIC Southeast Asia's senior communications officer.

J The Bird Conservation Society of Thailand has seen the number of helmeted hornbills depleted over the past 40 years by deforestation and climate change. "If we let the poaching goes on, it will wipe out the entire species in Thailand in no time." Kaset said. "They have to survive and have a better life if they are to refrain from cutting trees, and poaching. Without cooperation from people, no conservation plan will last long." said Thon Thamrongnawasawat, a respected government consultant on conservation and development.

(423 words)

Notes

1. Helmeted Hornbill:盔犀鸟(学名:Rhinoplax vigil)。它是所有犀鸟科鸟类中属于体型非常大的,因其巨大的喙上面那形状特别的盔突,整体是红色,平面部分为黄色,质地与象牙相似,制成的各种工艺品被广泛收藏,被称为鹤顶红。它被列入《濒危野生动植物国际贸易公约》(CITES)附录Ⅰ,相当于中国的国家一级保护动物。

2. International Union for Conservation of Nature:国际自然保护联盟。简称IUCN,是世界上规模最大、历史最悠久的全球性非营利环保机构。1999年,联合国授予其官方观察员的身份。

3. Kasetsart University:泰国农业大学。成立于1943年,是泰国知名大学之一。

4. TRAFFIC:国际野生物贸易研究组织。创建于1976年,是由WWF(世界自然基金会)与IUCN(世界自然保护联盟)合作支持成立的野生物贸易研究项目,其目标通过对全球野生动植物贸易的监测,保证贸易不危及野生动植物的生存。

Words

1. dwindling　n. 减少,缩小
2. exotic　adj. 外来的;异国情调的;奇异的
　　　　　n. 外国人;外来词
3. casque　n. 盔
4. atop　adv. 在顶上
　　　　prep. 在……的顶上
5. extinct　adj. 灭绝的;熄灭的;已死的
6. deploy　vt. 部署;使展开;施展
　　　　　vi. 展开
7. pendant　n. 垂饰;悬挂物
　　　　　adj. 下垂的;悬而未决的(＝pendent)
8. intensify　vt. 增强,强化,使尖锐
　　　　　　vi. 加强,变尖锐
9. avian　adj. 鸟类的
10. petition　n. 请愿书;祈求;申请
　　　　　　vi.(尤指用书面形式)请愿;祈求
　　　　　　vt. 向……请愿,正式请求
11. deplete　vt. 耗尽,使空竭
　　　　　　vi. 减少
12. refrain　vi. 抑制,自制以避免,克制
　　　　　　vt. 克制
　　　　　　n. 副歌;叠句;一再重复的话

Useful Expressions

1. critically endangered 极危物种
2. wildlife trade 野生动物交易
3. black market prices 黑市价格
4. conservation plan 保护方案

Difficult Sentences

1. Time is running out for Thailand's dwindling population of helmeted hornbills thanks to poaching of the exotic birds for the ivory-like casques atop their big red and yellow beaks.

本句的 thanks to 有讽刺的意味,说明的是灰犀鸟濒临灭绝的原因。

译文:由于偷猎这种奇异鸟类红黄相间鸟喙上类似象牙的盔突,留给数量逐渐减少的泰国犀鸟的时间已不多了。

2. Worries over the species' survival intensified after the wildlife trade monitoring

group TRAFFIC recently posted photos online of dozens of skulls of the endangered avian for sale.

本句的主句是"Worries...intensified",after 引导时间状语从句。

译文:在野生物贸易监控机构——国际野生物贸易研究组织最近在网络上公布了几十个贩卖的濒危鸟类头骨之后,他们对物种生存现状的担心更强了。

Reading Comprehension

There are five statements attached to the passage containing information given in one of the paragraphs. Identify the paragraph from which the information is derived and each paragraph is marked with a letter. You may only choose one paragraph once. Write down the letter in the blanks of each statement.

_____ 1. Helmeted hornbill is on the "critically endangered" list set by the International Union for Conservation of Nature.

_____ 2. The helmeted hornbills' casques are called red ivory in the illegal wildlife market.

_____ 3. Only with the cooperation from people we can protect the endangered birds and successfully carry the conservation plan.

_____ 4. If the birds were on the Wildlife Preservation List, government will give money, officers, tools as well as a national conservation plan for this species.

_____ 5. The distinctive casques of helmeted hornbills are made as decorative jewels, like rings and pendants.

Reading and Discussion

1. What caused the reducing in the population of helmeted hornbill?
2. Why did the campaign on change.org online site make a petition?
3. What is the most important factor to handle this problem that Thon Thamrongnawasawat suggested?

Language in Use

Complete each sentence with a word listed below. Make changes where necessary.

| exotic   extinct   intensify   dwindling   refrain |

1. Some birds are _____ and disappearing in the world due to the destruction of the wild environment.

2. The change of climate and the lost of forests are the main reasons that the number of helmeted hornbills has kept _____ over the past 40 years.

3. People's worries are _____ because of the hunting of helmeted hornbills for their casque atop.

4. The government in Thailand decided to take measures to protect endangered birds by _____ from cutting trees and poaching.

5. Some species are _____ from other places and they seem to be more adaptive to the environment than the local ones.

Reading 3

Indonesia Province Shuts Schools as Haze from Fires Returns
印尼行政区因大火烟雾致学校停课

October 14, 2019 (*China Daily*)

A PALEMBANG, Indonesia — Thick, noxious haze from new deliberately set fires blanketed parts of Indonesia's Sumatra island on Monday after days of improving air quality, causing school closings and flight delays. Haze from Indonesian fires, often set to clear land for planting, is an annual problem for Southeast Asia.

B National Disaster Mitigation Agency spokesman Agus Wibowo said nearly 1,200 fires were burning, more than double the number in past weeks as authorities managed to seed clouds to induce rain in several affected areas on Sumatra and Borneo islands.

C Wibowo said South Sumatra province had the largest number of detected fires, with nearly 700 hotspots, prompting authorities to shut most schools in Palembang, the province's capital, to protect children.

D Ari Subandri, the general manager of Airnav Indonesia in Palembang, said poor visibility caused delays at the city's main airport. Haze from Indonesian fires is often set to clear land for planting, is an annual problem for Southeast Asia.

E The fires are often started by smallholders and plantation owners to clear land for planting. Many areas of Indonesia are prone to rapid burning because of the draining of swampy peat land forests for pulp wood and palm oil plantations.

F Wibowo said seven helicopters dropped 66 million liters (17.4 million gallons) of water on Monday over South Sumatra province. He said firefighting measures included 14 tons of salt to induce rain in anticipation of worsening fires.

G This year alone, at least 52 helicopters have dropped more than 371 million liters (98 million gallons) of water and 255 tons of salt for cloud seeding as part of the firefighting efforts in six provinces that have declared emergencies. The provinces have a combined population of more than 23 million.

H Record Indonesian forest fires in 2015 spread haze across a swath of Southeast Asia, and according to a study by Harvard and Columbia universities, hastened 100,000 deaths.

(208 words)

>>> Notes

1. Palembang: 巨港市。原称旧港，又称巴邻旁，是印度尼西亚南苏门答腊省首府，苏门答腊岛第二大城市，也是东南亚最古老的城市之一。

2. Sumatra island: 苏门答腊岛。印度尼西亚西部的一个大型岛屿，是世界第六大

Chapter 8　Environment 环境

岛屿,也是印度尼西亚独自拥有的最大的岛屿。

3. Pekanbaru:北干巴鲁市。印度尼西亚廖内省省会和苏门答腊岛上第三大城市,位于苏门答腊岛中段,是廖内省重要港口及鱼产品市场。

4. Riau province:廖内省。印度尼西亚一级行政区。位于苏门答腊岛东部,东临马六甲海峡,与马来半岛隔海相望。

5. National Disaster Mitigation Agency:印尼国家减灾机构,是印尼灾害预防与救援的主要负责机构。

6. Borneo islands:婆罗洲岛,是世界第三大岛,亚洲第一大岛,也是世界上独一无二的分属于三个国家(印度尼西亚、文莱和马来西亚)的岛屿。

7. Airnav Indonesia:印尼国家航线运作公司。印尼一家规模较大的航空运输公司。

Words

1. noxious　adj. 有害的,有毒的
2. extinguish　vt. 熄灭,扑灭;消灭;使破灭;压制
3. peat land　n. 泥炭地
4. regency　n. 摄政统治;摄政期间;摄政权
　　　　　adj. 摄政的
5. detect　v. 发觉,察觉;查明,测出
6. hotspot　n. 热点
7. smallholder　n. 小农,小佃农
8. swampy　adj. 沼泽似的;沼泽的
9. swath　n. 割刈的带状地;长而宽的一长条
10. hasten　vt. 催促,使赶快;加速
　　　　　vi. 赶快

Useful Expressions

1. seed clouds/cloud seeding 人工降雨
2. poor visibility 可视度低
3. firefighting measures 消防措施

Difficult Sentences

1. Thick, noxious haze from new deliberately set fires blanketed parts of Indonesia's Sumatra island on Monday after days of improving air quality, causing school closings and flight delays.

本句的主句是 Thick, noxious haze ... blanketed parts of Indonesia's Sumatra island on Monday,after 引导时间状语从句,causing school closings and flight delays 中现在分词作伴随性状语。

译文:在经历了几天空气质量改善之后,本周一因有人蓄意放火而产生的浓重有毒烟雾覆盖了印尼苏门答腊岛的部分地区,导致学校停课、飞机延误。

2. National Disaster Mitigation Agency spokesman Agus Wibowo said nearly 1,200 fires were burning, more than double the number in past weeks as authorities managed to seed clouds to induce rain in several affected areas on Sumatra and Borneo islands.

as 引导时间状语从句,表示"正当……",作为间接引语后的时间引导词。

译文:国家减灾机构发言人奥格斯·维博沃说道,当政府正努力在苏门答腊岛和婆罗洲岛的受灾地区人工降雨时,又发生了近1,200场大火,比过去几周的火灾数量多了两倍多。

Reading Comprehension

There are five statements attached to the passage containing information given in one of the paragraphs. Identify the paragraph from which the information is derived and each paragraph is marked with a letter. You may only choose one paragraph once. Write down the letter in the blanks of each statement.

_____ 1. Flights were delayed in Palembangdue to the poor visibility.

_____ 2. Six provinces in Indonesia have announced the situations as emergencies.

_____ 3. It is an annual problem for Southeast Aisa that Indonesian fires cause poisonous haze around the country.

_____ 4. The fires in this week were more than twice the number of last week and seed clouds were used to reduce the haze in Sumatra.

_____ 5. The fires in Indonesian were burning quickly because the swampy peat land forests were drained out.

Reading and Discussion

1. What problems did the recent fire haze affect ordinary life?
2. How seriously were the fires this time?
3. What cause the fire rapid burning?

Language in Use

Complete each sentence with a word listed below. Make changes where necessary.

noxious   extinguish   regency   detect   hasten

1. The toxic haze aroused the attention from Indonesian _____ and helicopters were put into use to drop more than 300 million liters of water.

2. The fire haze in Indonesia emitted _____ gas around the affected area.

3. When the fire number in this week has been doubled, the authority urged the Firefighting Bureau to _____ their measures to cease the fire.

4. The firefighting measures were implemented including cloud seeding in order to _____ fires in the city.

5. The fires in Indonesia were mostly _____ as the smallholders and plantation owners were clearing the lands for the next year's planting.

Chapter 9 Tourism

旅游

ASEAN

Reading 1

Thai Tourism Targets 10 Percent Growth for 60th Anniversary
泰国旅游业将在60周年之际实现10%的增长目标

July 9, 2019 (*People's Daily*)

A   In preparation for its 60th anniversary next year, the Tourism Authority of Thailand (TAT) reaffirmed commitments to making travel to the country economically promising, sustainable, and vibrant.

B   TAT Governor Yuthasak Supasorn said the completion of the country's 5th cycle will be a time for reflection on past achievements and while looking forward to a new era filled with challenges.

C   "With the positive outcome in 2018, Thai tourism has clearly succeeded in fulfilling its mandate." Supasorn said.

"We will work even harder to maintain our brand image, preserve our competitive advantages, and ensure that the socio-economic benefits of international and domestic tourism are spread right across the country." he added.

D   The TAT initiative will align its strategies with the National Economic and Social Development Board, Thailand's national planning agency, whose Secretary General, Thosaphorn Sirisamphan, also serves as TAT Chairman.

E   2020 targets include boosting tourism revenue by 10 percent. TAT efforts will also see a shift in direction from a mass tourism mindset to responsible tourism with an emphasis on quality and revenue generating travel experiences.

F   Responsible tourism efforts will be featured in "Osotho," a new TAT in-house travel magazine.

G   "TAT will launch a nationwide campaign to mark its 60th anniversary with core messages highlighting the importance of responsible tourism and being good hosts under the theme of 'Next steps towards a sustainable Thailand'." said Supasorn.

H   The initiative will focus on TAT employees, the Thai people, and tourism stakeholders.

I   Meanwhile, "Amazing Thailand Week" will be planned for the international market by foreign TAT offices.

J   TAT efforts aimed at the domestic market will see travelers categorized in groups like Gen X, Gen Y, family and millennial family, silver age, ladies, first job, multi-gen, and corporate.

K   In foreign markets, TAT will focus on specific groups and middle-upper income brackets. It will seek first-time visitors in new and long-standing source markets. It will also attempt to balance out the seasonality factor and generate more demand in the "Green Season".

L   Other features will also be developed such as, homestays, walking paths, and local cuisine. Digital technology will be implemented to reach more customers.

M The marketing campaign, "Open to the New Shades," will direct attention to providing positive travel experiences. Following the long-standing "Amazing Thailand" slogan, future advertising campaigns will continue to target specific groups while highlighting Thai friendliness and hospitality.

N "Next year is likely to be a test due to the impact of international developments, global geopolitical friction, and economic difficulties, increasing competition, a relatively strong Baht, and reduced spending power." said Supasorn.

O However, the governor remains optimistic as the global travel and tourism market remains vibrant throughout the Asia-Pacific region.

(438 words)

Notes

1. Tourism Authority of Thailand (TAT):泰国国家旅游局。泰国旅游局是促进泰国旅游业发展的领军者,并致力于将泰国打造成为最受欢迎的旅游目的地。
2. National Economic and Social Development Board 国民经济和社会发展委员会。
3. Osotho:泰国旅游局出版的旅游杂志,提供泰国旅游景点、泰国美食、泰国节日等众多旅游资讯。
4. Baht:泰铢,泰国的官方货币。
5. Gen X, Gen Y(Generation X,Generation Y):X一代,Y一代。X一代指出生于20世纪60年代中期到20世纪80年代初的一代人;Y一代指从20世纪80年代初到20世纪90年代中期之间出生的人。

Words

1. anniversary   n.周年纪念日
2. commitment   n.献身,投入;承诺
3. sustainable   adj.能持续的,能保持的;能承受的
4. vibrant   adj.充满活力的,活跃的;震动的,颤抖的
           n.浊音
5. achievement   n.成功,成就;实现
6. mandate   n.命令,指令;执政权;委任
           vt.批准,颁布
7. align   vt.使成一线;使结盟;排整齐
         vi.成一直线;结盟
8. stakeholder   n.股东;参股者
9. categorize   vt.将……进行分类
10. attempt   vt.试图做
             n.尝试,努力;攻击
11. optimistic   adj.乐观的,乐观主义的

Chapter 9　Tourism 旅游

Useful Expressions

1. global geopolitical friction 全球地缘政治摩擦
2. spending power 购买力
3. friendliness and hospitality 友善与好客
4. the global travel and tourism market 全球旅游市场
5. millennial family 千禧年家庭

Difficult Sentences

1. "We will work even harder to maintain our brand image, preserve our competitive advantages, and ensure that the socio-economic benefits of international and domestic tourism are spread right across the country." he added.

本句中 to 引导两个目的性状语 maintain... advantages 和 and ensure... country。that the socio-economic benefits of international and domestic tourism are spread right across the country 是宾语从句做 ensure 的宾语。

译文:"我们会更加努力地维护我们的品牌形象,保持我们的竞争优势,并确保国家在国际和国内旅游业中会获得社会经济利益。"他补充说。

2. "Next year is likely to be a test due to the impact of international developments, global geopolitical friction, and economic difficulties, increasing competition, a relatively strong Baht, and reduced spending power." said Supasorn.

本句中 due to 引导原因状语从句。Next year is likely to be a test 是主句,句子用表达时间的词 next year 作为主语,强调 next year 的重要性。

译文:Supasorn 说:"由于受国际形势、全球地缘政治摩擦、经济困难、竞争加剧、泰铢相对坚挺和消费能力下降的影响,明年可能会是一个考验。"

Reading Comprehension

There are five statements attached to the passage containing information given in one of the paragraphs. Identify the paragraph from which the information is derived and each paragraph is marked with a letter. You may only choose one paragraph once. Write down the letter in the blanks of each statement.

_____ 1. The goal of TAT in 2020 is to promote the tourism revenue growth by 10 percent.

_____ 2. A campaign across the nation which focuses on the significance of responsible tourism will be implemented to celebrate the 60th anniversary.

_____ 3. It is a time for TAT to learn lesson from the previous achievements and expect next challenging era.

_____ 4. The governor holds a positive attitude towards Thai tourism because the vigorous and active global travel and tourism market in the Asia-Pacific region.

_____ 5. At home market some specific groups from Gen X, Gen Y, family and millennial family to silver age, ladies, first job, multi-gen, and corporate are the targets of TAT.

▶▶▶ Reading and Discussion

1. What's responsible tourism?
2. What's the focus of TAT efforts at the domestic and foreign markets?
3. What's the attitude of the governor towards the Thai tourism in 2020?

▶▶▶ Language in Use

Complete each sentence with a word listed below. Make changes where necessary.

sustainable vibrant align mandate attempt

1. Domestic prices have been _____ with those in world market.
2. The creation of an efficient and _____ transport system is critical.
3. The prisoners _____ to escape, but failed.
4. The election victory gave the party a clear _____ to continue its programme of its reform.
5. Thailand is the most _____ place during the New Year celebrations.

Reading 2

Cambodia Unveils Masterplan to Boost Tourism in 2 World Heritage Sites
柬埔寨公布振兴两处世界遗产旅游的总体规划

September 26, 2019 (Xinhua. net)

A   Cambodia is set to roll out the Four-Strategic Plan for Tourism Development aimed at reviving tourism at the Angkor Archaeological Park and the Preah Vihear temple in northern provinces, a local newspaper reported on Wednesday.

B   The two main tourist destinations saw a 9.7 percent and 5.5 percent drop in tourists during the first seven months of this year.

C   Tourism Minister Thong Khon and Environment Minister Say Samal unveiled the masterplan for tourism development in the northern provinces during an inter-ministerial committee meeting on Monday, the Phnom Penh Post reported.

D   The four-strategic plan includes diversifying new tourism products and extending the stay of tourists, boosting competitiveness, improving connectivity and crafting a new identity for the "Siem Reap area" which includes Preah Vihear province.

E   Khon said that development of new tourism products is necessary to attract tourists to the two world heritage sites, the Angkor Archaeological Park in Siem Reap province and the Preah Vihear temple in Preah Vihear province.

F   "We are currently working actively to make Cambodia a quality tourist destination, meaning that apart from efforts to strengthen services, the sale of fake products to cheat tourists must also be stopped." he was quoted as saying by the Phnom

Chapter 9 Tourism 旅游

Penh Post.

G He said the authorities would not allow the sale of counterfeit souvenirs and jewelry to continue as it causes a significant impact on Cambodia's tourism destinations and national prestige as a whole.

H During the meeting, the committee also designated the Tonle Sap Lake area, Kulen Mountain, Siem Reap town and surrounding areas as zones for new tourism product development.

I Tourist arrivals dropped by 9.7 percent year-on-year in Siem Reap province in the first seven months of this year and rose 27.9 percent year-on-year in Phnom Penh, a Ministry of Tourism report shows.

J Tourist arrivals in coastal areas climbed 31.9 percent year-on year during the same period and increased 9.4 percent year-on-year in ecotourism areas, it shows.

K The report said that in the first seven months of this year, Cambodia welcomed 3.84 million foreign tourists, up 11.1 percent on the same period last year.

L The number of Chinese tourists reached 1.5 million during the period, up 37 percent year-on-year, Vietnamese tourists hit nearly 480,000, up 4.6 percent year-on-year, and Lao tourists were nearly 220,000, down 1.9 percent.

(375 words)

Notes

1. Angkor Archaeological Park：柬埔寨吴哥考古公园，也叫吴哥窟。1992年，联合国教科文组织把整个吴哥古迹列为世界文化遗产，即吴哥考古公园。
2. Preah Vihear temple：柏威夏寺，其复杂的历史可追溯到9世纪。柏威夏寺矗立在峭壁上，俯瞰整个柬埔寨平原。由于地处偏远，地形险要，柏威夏寺保存得相当完好。
3. Siem Reap：柬埔寨城市暹粒，是柬埔寨暹粒省的省会，吴哥窟就在暹粒。
4. Tonle Sap Lake：洞里萨湖，又名金边湖，位于柬埔寨境内西部，呈长条形位于柬埔寨的心脏地带，是东南亚最大的淡水湖泊。
5. Kulen Mountain：荔枝山，是柬埔寨佛教圣地和著名风景区。

Words

1. masterplan v. 根据总体规划设计
2. unveil vi. 揭去面纱，揭开蒙布；揭示
        vt. 向公众透露；揭去……的面纱
3. boost vt. 推动，推进；使增长
      vi. 做广告
      n. 推动，促进；一推；提高，增长
4. revive vt. 使复活，使苏醒
       vi. 复苏，复活，苏醒；复原
5. diversify vt. 使不同，使多样化

vi. 多样化

6. counterfeit   adj. 伪造的,仿造的;虚假的,假装的

n. 伪造物,赝品

vt. 伪造;假装

vi. 欺骗;从事(货币等)伪造活动

7. prestige   n. 声望,威望,威信

Useful Expressions

1. world heritage 世界遗产名录
2. quality tourist destination 优质旅游目的地
3. the sale of fake products 假冒产品的销售

Difficult Sentences

1. The four-strategic plan includes diversifying new tourism products and extending the stay of tourists, boosting competitiveness, improving connectivity and crafting a new identity for the "Siem Reap area" which includes Preah Vihear province.

本句中 diversifying, extending, boosting and improving 引导的动名词短语做 includes 的宾语。which includes Preah Vihear province 是定语从句修饰 the "Siem Reap area"。

译文:这四个战略计划包括使新的旅游产品多样化,延长游客停留时间,增强竞争力,改善互联互通,以及为包括柏威夏省在内的"暹粒地区"打造新的旅游名片。

2. "We are currently working actively to make Cambodia a quality tourist destination, meaning that apart from efforts to strengthen services, the sale of fake products to cheat tourists must also be stopped." he was quoted as saying by the Phnom Penh Post.

本句中的 to make Cambodia a quality tourist destination 是动词不定式短语做目的性状语,meaning that 做伴随性状语,相当于 It means that...。

译文:他引用金边邮报的说法,"我们目前正通过积极的努力,使柬埔寨成为一个优质的旅游目的地,这意味着除了努力加强服务外,还必须禁止销售假冒产品欺骗游客。"

Reading Comprehension

There are five statements attached to the passage containing information given in one of the paragraphs. Identify the paragraph from which the information is derived and each paragraph is marked with a letter. You may only choose one paragraph once. Write down the letter in the blanks of each statement.

_____ 1. Statistics in a Ministry of Tourism report shows that the number of tourists who visited Siem Reap province decreased by 9.7 percent year-on-year in the first seven month of this year.

_____ 2. To make Cambodia a quality tourist destination, some rules are put into effect to strengthen services, in addition, it is forbidden to sell counterfeit products.

_____ 3. It is reported by a local newspaper that the Four-Strategic Plan for Tourism Development will be launched to boost tourism.

_____ 4. It is essential for the two world heritage sites to design new tourism products to attract visitors.

_____ 5. The fame of Cambodia as a tourism destinations will be influenced if the authorities don't prohibit the sales of fake goods.

Reading and Discussion

1. Why did Cambodia unveil the Four-Strategic Plan for Tourism Development?
2. How will Cambodia create quality tourist destination for tourists?
3. What's the influence of the sale of fake products in Cambodia?

Language in Use

Complete each sentence with a word listed below. Make changes where necessary.

boost   prestige   revive   diversify   counterfeit

1. The economy is beginning to _____.
2. The movie helped _____ her screen career.
3. He admitted possessing and delivering _____ currency.
4. As demand has increased, manufacturers have been encouraged to _____ products and improve quality.
5. The _____ of the university influence employers' recruitment decisions.

Reading 3

Record-Breaking, 3740-feet-long Waterslide Opens in Malaysia
马来西亚的水上滑道开业

September 26, 2019(CNN)

A The downside to waterslides? The effort usually always exceeds the reward, at least where time's concerned.

B You climb dozens of steps to reach the slide's entry point, huffing and puffing your way to the top, only to find yourself floundering about in the exit pool mere seconds later.

C This won't be the case with a new waterslide that's just opened in Malaysia.

D Stretching a whopping 1,140 meters (3,740 feet) long, the ride snakes through the undergrowth at Penang's ESCAPE theme park is claimed to have smashed the previous record for world's longest tube waterslide held by Action Park, a theme park in

Vernon, New Jersey.

E Unlike the New Jersey version, which is inflatable, ESCAPE's new slide is made of fiber-reinforced polymer and is a permanent structure attached to steel poles.

F "Breaking the world record was never our intention," said Sim Choo Kheng, CEO of ESCAPE operator Sim Leisure Group, in a statement. "I'm always baffled by how rides are made so short and quick. I wanted to build rides that last a good few minutes."

G The slide offers a four-minute ride that meanders its way down a 70-meter slope, passing through jungle scenery.

H Huffing and puffing won't be part of the experience either. Visitors access the slide via a cable car chairlift.

I It brings the global spotlight to Penang. The island of Penang, off the western coast of Malaysia, is more famous for culture and cuisine than thrills.

J George Town, the island's main city, is its top draw thanks to a colorful mix of cultures that includes Hindu and Buddhist temples, street art, Islamic mosques, British colonial architecture and ornate Chinese manor houses.

K Penang is also considered one of the world's top food destinations, thanks to the presence of delicious Malay, Chinese and Indian cuisine that includes dishes like Hokkien mee (fried prawn noodles) and Penang laksa.

L ESCAPE is about 30 minutes from George Town and offers a variety of adventure activities including waterslides, ziplines and obstacle courses.

(327 words)

Notes

1. Penang:槟城,马来西亚十三个联邦州之一,地处西马来西亚西北部,有"印度洋绿宝石"之称。槟城属热带雨林气候,著名景点有升旗山、极乐寺等。

2. George Town:乔治市,是槟城的首府,于2008年7月7日被联合国文教科组织列为世界文化遗产。

Words

1. flounder   v. 无助地挣扎,蹒跚;思绪紊乱;心乱如麻
             n. 鲆;鲽;挣扎;踉跄
2. smash   vt. 猛力打碎;猛撞;压扁
          vi. 被打破;被粉碎
          adv. 哗啦一响
          adj. (口)轰动一时的
3. inflatable   adj. 可充气的
               n. 可充气物
4. permanent   adj. 永久的,永恒的;持久的
              n. 烫发

5. baffle　vt. 使困惑；使受挫折；阻隔

　　　　　vi. 徒作挣扎

　　　　　n. 困惑；障碍

6. meander　vi. 蜿蜒延伸；漫步，蹓跶

　　　　　　vt. 沿着（河流等）迂回曲折地前进

　　　　　　n. 迷宫；徘徊，漫步

Useful Expressions

1. theme park 主题公园
2. a cable car chairlift 缆车索道
3. huffing and puffing 气喘吁吁地

Difficult Sentences

1. Stretching a whopping 1,111 meters (3,645 feet) long, the ride snakes through the undergrowth at Penang's ESCAPE theme park is claimed to have smashed the previous record for world's longest tube waterslide held by Action Park, a theme park in Vernon, New Jersey.

Stretching a whopping 1,111 meters (3,645 feet) long 在本句中做伴随性状语，意思为"蜿蜒1,111米长。"主干是 the ride snakes is claimed to...。held by Action Park 是过去分词做后置定语修饰 waterslide。

译文：蜿蜒长达1,111米（3645英尺），这条经过槟城Escape主题公园灌木丛的蛇形的水上滑道，声称打破了此前由新泽西州弗农市的一家行动主题公园创造的世界最长滑水道的纪录。

2. George Town, the island's main city, is its top draw thanks to a colorful mix of cultures that includes Hindu and Buddhist temples, street art, Islamic mosques, British colonial architecture and ornate Chinese manor houses.

本句中 that includes... 是定语从句修饰 cultures。

译文：岛上的主要城市乔治市，由于其丰富多彩的文化，包括印度教和佛教寺庙，街头艺术，伊斯兰清真寺，英国殖民时期的建筑和华丽的中国庄园，成为岛上最吸引人的地方。

Reading Comprehension

There are five statements attached to the passage containing information given in one of the paragraphs. Identify the paragraph from which the information is derived and each paragraph is marked with a letter. You may only choose one paragraph once. Write down the letter in the blanks of each statement.

　　　　　1. George Town, the main attraction of the island, is famous for its culture diversity.

　　　　　2. The difference between the New Jersey version and ESCAPE's new slide is that the former is inflatable while the latter is a permanent structure.

_____ 3. As one of the world's top food destination, various kinds of delicious food from different countries can be tasted in Pennang.

_____ 4. By riding through jungle scenery, it will take four minutes for the slide to wind its way down from 70-meter slope.

_____ 5. The slide in Escape theme park broke the world's longest tube waterslide record kept by a theme park in New Jersey.

》》》 Reading and Discussion

1. What's the difference between the waterslide in New Jersey version and ESCAPE's new slide?

2. What is Penang well-known for?

3. What's the intention of building world's longest tube waterslide, according to CEO of ESCAPE operator?

》》》 Language in Use

Complete each sentence with a word listed below. Make changes where necessary.

smash   permanent   baffle   meander   flounder

1. We _____ through a landscape of mountains, rivers, and vineyards.

2. The demonstrators used trucks to _____ through embassy gates.

3. Right now, you've got a president who's _____, trying to find some way to get his campaign jump-started.

4. Sometimes the decisions _____ and enrage me.

5. Heavy drinking can cause _____ damage to the brain.

Keys
参考答案

Chapter 1

Reading 1

Reading Comprehension

1. E   2. B   3. C   4. A   5. D

Reading and Discussion

1. ASEAN also promotes political stability in individual countries and encourages collaboration on matters of mutual concern.

2. ASEAN established a free trade area.

3. The institutionalization of visa-free travel in the ASEAN region has promoted inter-ASEAN travel and hence tourism.

Language in Use

1. established
2. promote
3. mutual
4. accelerate
5. comprise

Reading 2

Reading Comprehension

1. F   2. C   3. A   4. E   5. B

Reading and Discussion

1. He affirmed that ASEAN will continue working to ensure the sustainable supply of sufficient, safe and nutritious food that meet the dietary requirements of ASEAN populations during and after the outbreak of the COVID-19.

2. The AMAF promised to minimize disruptions in regional food supply chains by working closely together to ensure that markets are kept open and transportation of agricultural and food products are facilitated.

3. The study will provide recommendations and advice to all AMS on how to address these challenges effectively.

Language in Use

1. implement
2. outbreak
3. mitigate
4. pledge
5. sustainable

Reading 3
Reading Comprehension
1. D 2. B 3. C 4. F 5. A

Reading and Discussion
1. To mainstream the rights of persons with disabilities.
2. They highlighted universal design as precondition to enabling environment and the need for public-private-people partnership with participation of persons with disabilities and organisations of persons with disabilities to ensure accessibility and inclusion.
3. Three days.

Language in Use
1. underlines
2. highlight
3. participant
4. foster
5. commenced

Chapter 2
Reading 1
Reading Comprehension
1. H 2. E 3. F 4. A 5. B

Reading and Discussion
1. Jakarta
2. Due to over-extraction of groundwater and the location of this city.
3. Because of a worsening air pollution crisis, exacerbated by near-constant traffic congestion on its roads.

Language in Use
1. dire
2. congested
3. exacerbate
4. governance
5. myriad

Reading 2
Reading Comprehension
1. G 2. H 3. D 4. F 5. B

Reading and Discussion

1. It was hacked involving its e-pay portal.

2. He thinks that the current law is enforceable, but at the same time we need to look at how we can implement amendments to strengthen and tighten existing laws to meet the challenges and threats we face today.

3. They provide training opportunities and content for micro and youth entrepreneurs to gain knowledge in digital entrepreneurship including marketing through social media, e-marketplaces, data analysis, online payments, digital advertising and cyber security.

Language in Use
1. referred
2. implemented
3. enforceable
4. accelerate
5. provision

Reading 3
Reading Comprehension
1. A   2. B   3. D   4. F   5. C

Reading and Discussion
1. Ten trees.
2. The Philippines has lost more than 30% of its forest cover due to illegal logging.
3. One school in India made its students pay their "school fees" by collecting, bringing to school, and recycling plastic waste that was lying across the town.

Language in Use
1. indigenous
2. foster
3. reverse
4. forefront
5. initiative

Chapter 3
Reading 1
Reading Comprehension
1. A   2. D   3. F   4. H   5. L

Reading and Discussion

1. Reasons are as follows:

① To cushion the impact of the global economic downturn.

② To bolster trade within Asia to compensate for falling demand in the West due to the plummeting exports from Southeast Asia.

③ To expand Trade among the 10 members of the ASEAN.

2. This week's Leaders Summit would push harder for the realization of a common market by 2015.

3. We shall no longer be running around following the other advanced economies, and lead the world out of this crisis and I think we can do it because we are better cushioned than before.

Language in Use
1. downturn
2. Plummeting
3. accelerate
4. integration
5. bolster

Reading 2
Reading Comprehension
1. D 2. J 3. B 4. H 5. C

Reading and Discussion

1. They are trying to ensure price stability and sustainable growth in the medium term.

2. This means that the government has taken out less revenue than it is spending.

3. The constraints such as policy space, debt sustainability and financial stability concerns could cap the stimulus to these economies.

Language in Use
1. reiterated
2. expansionary
3. revenue
4. sustainability
5. stimulatory

Reading 3
Reading Comprehension
1. I   2. D   3. G   4. K   5. B

Reading and Discussion
1. The law will hurt the economy and further restrict freedom of expression.
2. This is necessary for the country's cybersecurity and will facilitate the companies' operations and user activities.
3. She urged them to use the considerable power they have at their disposal to challenge Viet Nam's government on this legislation.

Language in Use
1. localization
2. facilitate
3. refuge
4. treazies
5. censure

Chapter 4
Reading 1
Reading Comprehension
1. E   2. C   3. B   4. H   5. I

Reading and Discussion
1. The Singapore Police Force has issued a warning to residents not to "misuse" their boarding passes.
2. Because the misuse of boarding passes is an offense in Singapore, where transit areas are considered "protected places".
3. It made headlines around the globe for its 40-meter waterfall (the world's largest indoor one), a 14,000-square-meter Canopy Park, completed with a suspension bridge, topiary and mazes, and one of Asia's largest indoor gardens with 3,000 trees and 60,000 shrubs.

Language in Use
1. forged
2. offense
3. odd
4. legislation
5. on-site

Reading 2
Reading Comprehension
1. B 2. D 3. G 4. E 5. F

Reading and Discussion
1. Indonesia has pledged to reduce plastic waste in its waters some 70 percent by 2025 by boosting recycling, raising public awareness, and curbing usage.
2. An hour-long bus ride with unlimited stops costs three large bottles, five medium bottles or 10 plastic cups. But they must be cleaned and cannot be squashed.
3. Bali is phasing in a ban on single-use plastic straws and bags to rid the popular holiday island of waste choking its waterways, while authorities in the capital Jakarta are considering a similar bylaw to rid the city of plastic shopping bags.

Language in Use
1. phased
2. transit
3. roam
4. pledge
5. equivalent

Reading 3
Reading Comprehension
1. J 2. I 3. A 4. G 5. E

Reading and Discussion
1. The law came into force on August 20.
2. Because scientific studies show that passive smokers are at greater risk of being affected by cancer.
3. Once convicted, the court may order a person to receive treatment to quit smoking in an attempt to protect the person's family.

Language in Use
1. initiate
2. exceed
3. reside
4. convicted
5. unwittingly

Chapter 5

Reading 1

Reading Comprehension

1. M   2. F   3. N   4. A   5. G

Reading and Discussion

1. The telecom regulator may have to consider providing financial assistance for mobile operators or introducing an infrastructure-sharing scheme for mobile operators or introducing an infrastructure-sharing scheme to ease the financial burden shouldered by operators.

2. Drones, remote-controlled vehicles, robotics, smart homes, smart factories, smart farms and smart healthcare are expected to be the first tier of 5G use cases, according to analysts.

3. The company plans to offer 5G Fixed Wireless Access Internet service under its DTAC@Home project, competing with the fibre-optic high-speed network.

Language in Use

1. catering
2. innovative
3. artificial
4. accessed
5. intelligence

Reading 2

Reading Comprehension

1. J   2. L   3. A   4. G   5. B

Reading and Discussion

1. Local technology players, industry associations and tech agencies in general applaud the various allocations set aside towards making Malaysia a stronger player and contender in the technology arena, both locally and abroad.

2. 100 Go Digital has been launched to enable traditional Malaysian businesses to embrace digitization.

3. MDEC will also continue to manage and improve its Digital Transformation Acceleration Program.

Language in Use

1. budget
2. applauded
3. empower

4. access

5. ecosystems

Reading 3
Reading Comprehension
1. E   2. G   3. A   4. C   5. B

Reading and Discussion
1. Alipay announced the conclusion of the first "cashless" trip made by Chinese visitors to Singapore, together with the Singapore Tourism Board (STB).

2. SBT hopes to use the insights from this initiative to explore better ways of engaging Chinese visitors and to offer more compelling and seamless experiences through Alipay that are better tailored to their passions.

3. Because the Chinese market is the top source market for both visitor arrivals and tourist spending for Singapore.

Language in Use
1. cashless
2. demonstrate
3. statistics
4. purchased
5. compelling

Chapter 6
Reading 1
Reading Comprehension
1. F   2. E   3. G   4. I   5. B

Reading and Discussion
1. He wanted to help students who missed class for competing in the junior college sometimes keep up with their studies.

2. Students can access material such as quizzes and tutorial videos on their mobile phones from the app, and the app allows teachers to use a hashtag function from which they can retrieve saved comments, to customize it to students' needs. Hence students can benefit from the more substantive feedback.

3. Economics alone cannot solve the challenges of the allocation and distribution of resources in society, but a good understanding of the subject can help design schemes to effectively redistribute resources.

Language in Use
1. redistributed
2. refined
3. feedback
4. customize
5. frustrated

Reading 2
Reading Comprehension
1. E 2. F 3. A 4. J 5. H

Reading and Discussion
1. The shortage of surgeons in Malaysia, because a growing elderly population and trends towards increased healthcare utilization had contributed to a higher demand for the profession.
2. The RCSEd's International Strategy is aimed to promote the surgery as a career of choice among medical practitioners.
3. To be a surgeon one needs to have a lot of stamina to deal with those physically demanding in terms of daily routines in managing patients and performing practical procedures at all times of the day, and one needs to be technically excellent and pose good academic knowledge.

Language in Use
1. draft
2. address
3. demanding
4. collaboration
5. pursue

Reading 3
Reading Comprehension
1. O 2. H 3. N 4. B 5. E

Reading and Discussion
1. According to Ramon del Rosario, Shell hopes to inspire a generation of innovative Filipino scientists, thinkers, mentors, city planners and decision-makers through The Bright Ideas Challenge.
2. 26 teams submitted entries on how to sustainably power future cities.
3. The student team from Philippine Science High School Cagayan Valley (Team

Pisay CVC) won the grand prize.

Language in Use
1. principles
2. tackle
3. curiosity
4. external
5. spark

Chapter 7

Reading 1
Reading Comprehension
1. G 2. D 3. I 4. K 5. H

Reading and Discussion
1. To encourage Singaporeans to speak Mandarin.
2. Mandarin has helped unify Singapore's Chinese community, strengthening kinship and enabling a deeper understanding of Singapore's Chinese culture.
3. These terms are used in Singapore but may not be commonly used in other Mandarin speaking regions.

Language in Use
1. bilingual
2. launched
3. ascribe
4. unify
5. kinship

Reading 2
Reading Comprehension
1. D 2. N 3. B 4. C 5. A

Reading and Discussion
1. Foreigners.
2. Vietnam has continued to experience income growth and taste for global concepts and standards. The tastes and preferences of Vietnamese consumers are changing and evolving.
3. Craft beer will be their favorite beer. They prefer craft beer to traditional lagers.

Language in Use
1. infuse
2. booming
3. alternative
4. potent
5. evolve

Reading 3
Reading Comprehension
1. C 2. A 3. G 4. E 5. F

Reading and Discussion
1. Because of the impact of COVID-19.
2. They hastily made homework assignments without knowing how long the schools would be closed.
3. They lacked the tech to learn from home. They have complained that it is ineffective.

Language in Use
1. assign
2. disparities
3. underfunded
4. complained
5. access

Chapter 8
Reading 1
Reading Comprehension
1. G 2. B 3. D 4. J 5. E

Reading and Discussion
1. They are similar to the other well-studied ecosystems, such as seawater, soil and the human gut.
2. This ability can provides us:
①insights into many aspects of urban life that affect our daily living and human well-being.
②an understanding of the interactions between atmospheric, terrestrial and aquatic planetary ecosystems.
3. The previous study failed in achieving a temporal resolution that would have allowed for observing the daily cycling of airborne microorganisms.

Language in Use
1. respiratory
2. microorganisms
3. bacteria
4. temporal
5. aggregates

Reading 2
Reading Comprehension
1. B   2. H   3. J   4. G   5. D

Reading and Discussion
1. It is due to the poaching of the exotic birds for the ivory-like casques atop their big red and yellow beaks.
2. It was pressuring the government to add the bird to Thailand's Wildlife Preservation List as soon as possible.
3. The cooperation from people is the key factor.

Language in Use
1. extinct
2. dwindling
3. intensified
4. refraining
5. exotic

Reading 3
Reading Comprehension
1. E   2. H   3. A   4. C   5. F

Reading and Discussion
1. It caused school closings and flight delays.
2. Nearly 1,200 fires were burning, more than double the number in past weeks.
3. The fires are often started by smallholders and plantation owners to clear land for planting, and the draining of swampy peat land forests for pulp wood and palm oil plantations made them rapid burning.

Language in Use

1. regency

2. noxious

3. hasten

4. extinguish

5. detected

Chapter 9

Reading 1

Reading Comprehension

1. E 2. G 3. B 4. O 5. J

Reading and Discussion

1. Responsible tourism emphasizes on quality and revenue generating travel experiences.

2. At the domestic markets, it focuses on travelers categorized in groups like Gen X, Gen Y, family and millennial family, silver age, ladies, first job, multi-gen, and corporate.

At the foreign markets, it focuses on specific groups and middle-upper income brackets.

3. They are Optimistic about Thai Tourism in 2020.

Language in Use

1. aligned

2. sustainable

3. attempted

4. mandate

5. vibrant

Reading 2

Reading Comprehension

1. I 2. F 3. A 4. E 5. G

Reading and Discussion

1. It aimed at reviving tourism at the Angkor Archaeological Park and the Preah Vihear temple in northern provinces.

2. The authority will make efforts to strengthen services and stop the sale of fake products to cheat tourists.

3. It causes a significant impact on Cambodia's tourism destinations and national prestige as a whole.

Language in Use
1. revive
2. boost
3. counterfeit
4. diversify
5. prestige

Reading 3
Reading Comprehension
1. J   2. E   3. K   4. G   5. D

Reading and Discussion
1. The New Jersey version is inflatable, while ESCAPE's new slide is made of fiber-reinforced polymer and is a permanent structure attached to steel poles.
2. It is famous for culture and food.
3. He wanted to build rides that last a good few minutes.

Language in Use
1. meandered
2. smash
3. floundering
4. baffle
5. permanent

Appendix Ⅰ

附录Ⅰ

ASEAN

东盟国家、首都及重要城市英语表达

▶▶▶ 东盟（东南亚国家联盟）ASEAN = Association of Southeast Asian Nations

▶▶▶ 印度尼西亚共和国 Republic of Indonesia
  雅加达市 Jakarta City 印度尼西亚首都和国内最大城市。
  泗水市 Surabaya City 东爪哇省省会和省内最大城市，东南亚最早的港口城市之一。
  万隆市 Bandung City 印度尼西亚第三大城市，西爪哇省首府。
  棉兰市 Medan City 印度尼西亚北苏门答腊省省会以及省内最大城市。
  日惹市 Yogyakarta City 一个有数百年历史的古城，是印度尼西亚境内唯一仍实行君主自治的区域，市内的苏丹皇宫住着苏丹王及其家属，也是印度尼西亚工业较发达的地区之一。

▶▶▶ 马来西亚 Malaysia
  吉隆坡市 Kuala Lumpur City 马来西亚的首都兼国内最大城市。
  槟城州 Penang Province 马来西亚北部的一个小州，包括了槟岛（Penang Island）和威省（Seberang Prai）。2008年7月7日槟城州首府乔治市被列入世界文化遗产名录。
  槟岛 Penang Island 又叫槟榔屿，著名的旅游胜地，被誉为"印度洋上的绿宝石""东方明珠"。
  马六甲市 Malacca City 马来西亚马六甲州的首府。2008年7月7日马六甲市被列入世界文化遗产名录。
  怡保市 Ipoh City 马来西亚霹雳州首府，工商业及交通中心，因当地盛产一种名叫"怡保"的有毒树木而得名。
  新山市 Johor Bahru City 马来西亚的柔佛州的首府，是马来西亚在马来半岛最南端，也是欧亚大陆最南端的城市，与邻国新加坡隔着柔佛海峡相对，有"马来西亚的南方门户"之称。
  兰卡威岛 Langkawi Island 一般指兰卡威群岛，马来西亚最大岛屿群，是马来西亚著名旅游景点之一。
  亚庇市 Kota Kinabalu City 是沙巴州和婆罗洲渔业的兴盛地、旅游景点，同时也是东马来西亚的工业及商业重镇，使得该市成为马来西亚发展最为快速的城市之一。

▶▶▶ 菲律宾共和国 Republic of the Philippines
  马尼拉市 Manila City 菲律宾首都及政府所在地，是东南亚最大城市之一。
  宿务市 Cebu City 菲律宾最古老的城市，也是菲律宾主要的港口和经济中心。
  达沃市 Davao City 菲律宾的第三大城市，也是其重要的经济中心。达沃是菲律宾南部棉兰老岛最大的港口和经济中心，全国蕉麻加工中心。

奎松市 Quezon City 其城市名来源于菲律宾第二任总统曼努埃尔·奎松,是菲律宾主要的经济、文化、政治和交通中心。

吕宋岛 Luzon Island 菲律宾北部的岛屿,菲律宾首都马尼拉位于该岛。

新加坡共和国 Republic of Singapore

新加坡市 Singapore City 新加坡共和国的首都,位于新加坡岛的南端。新加坡市是新加坡政治、经济、文化中心,有"花园城市"之称,是世界上最大港口之一和重要的国际金融中心。

圣淘沙岛 Sentosa Island 被誉为最迷人的新加坡度假小岛,有着多姿多彩的娱乐设施和休闲活动区域,素有"欢乐宝石"的美誉。

泰王国 The Kingdom of Thailand

曼谷市 Bangkok City 泰国首都和最大城市,别名"天使之城",东南亚第二大城市。

清迈市 Chiang Mai City 泰国第二大城市,清迈府首府,南亚著名的旅游胜地。

清莱府 Chiang Rai Province 泰国北部边境的府份。

普吉岛 Phuket Island 著名度假岛。

芭堤雅市 Pattaya City 著名海景度假胜地。

文莱达鲁萨兰国 Negara Brunei Darussalam

斯里巴加湾市 Bandar Seri Begawan 文莱首都。

越南社会主义共和国 Socialist Republic of Vietnam

河内市 Ha Noi City 越南的首都,越南第二大城市。

胡志明市 Ho Chi Minh City 越南的一个中央直辖市之一。

海防市 Hai Phong City 越南北部的沿海城市,越南的第三大城市。

岘港市 Da Nang City 越南中部滨海城市,天然良港,现为海军基地,也是美丽的度假胜地。

顺化市 Hue City 一座美丽的城市,承天顺化省省会,是越南的古都。

老挝人民民主共和国 The Lao People's Democratic Republic

万象市 Vientiane 老挝的首都和最大城市。

缅甸联邦共和国 The Republic of the Union of Myanmar

内比都市 Naypyidaw City 缅甸的首都。

仰光市 Yangon City 缅甸最大城市,也是最大的港口城市,东南亚最大港口之一。

勃生市 Pathein City 缅甸重要的港口城市,伊洛瓦底省省会。

曼德勒市 Mandalay City 缅甸第二大城市,位于缅甸中部,是古代王朝曾几度建都的地方,也是华侨聚集的城市。

密支那市 Myitkyina City 缅甸北部克钦邦首府,是缅甸北部最重要的港口城市。

柬埔寨王国 Kingdom of Cambodia

金边市 Phnom Penh City 柬埔寨首都和最大城市，为柬埔寨政治、经济、文化、交通、贸易中心。

马德望市 Battambang City 柬埔寨马德望省首府，全国第二大城市。

暹粒市 Siem Reap City 柬埔寨暹粒省的省会，是世界七大奇迹之一的吴哥窟所在地。

西哈努克市 Preah Sihanouk City 西哈努克省的省会，是柬埔寨的一个港口城市，同时也是比较热门的旅游胜地。

Appendix II

附录 II

ASEAN

新闻英语高频词汇

一、国际关系和外交政策

常见的考点：两国或多国之间的外交关系和各国政府的外交立场。

常用词汇

diplomatic relations 外交关系
envoy 外交使节,特使
break off 中断
recall 召回
strategic partnership 战略伙伴关系
economic sanction 经济制裁
unilateral 单边的
bilateral 双边的
multilateral 多边的
boycott 联合抵制

embargo 禁止(或限制)贸易令
interventionism(尤指主张干预国际事务的)干涉主义
embassy 大使馆
mediate 仲裁,调停,斡旋
consulate 领事馆
sovereignty 主权
ambassador 大使
autonomy 自治

二、国家领导人会晤和国际会议

常见的考点：出访人物、会谈对象、目的地、谈目标、议程和是否达成协议等细节。

常用词汇

convene 召开会议
lift 解除,撤销
multi-party talks 多方会谈
adjourn (会议)暂停,延期
peace talk 和平会谈
endorse 签署文件
summit 峰会
unanimously 全体一致地
convention 大会
consensus 一致,共识
Treaty on the Non-Proliferation of Nuclear Weapons《核不扩散条约》
Six-party Talks 六方会谈

forum 论坛
pact 公约,协定
turnout 出席人数
treaty 条约,谈判
venue (会议)地点
memorandum 备忘录
agenda 议程
ultimatum 最后通牒
suspend 中断
Geneva Convention 日内瓦公约
North American Free Trade Agreement 北美自由贸易协定

三、政治选举

常见的考点：候选人和政党名称，候选人的政治纲领、态度或构想，竞选活动，选票结果等。

常用词汇

referendum 公民投票

fundraising 筹款

general election 大选，普选
opinion poll 民意测验
primary 初选
approval rating 支持率
nominee 被提名人
ballot（无记名）选票
candidate 候选人
polling booth 投票站
opponent 对手

a landslide victory 压倒性的胜利
counselor 顾问
take the office 就职
constituency 全体选民
president-elect 当选而未就任的总统
platform（政党的）政治纲领
successor 继任者
campaign 竞选活动
settlement 定居地，殖民地，殖民

四、党派矛盾

常见的考点：党派的名称，政治观点产生分歧的原因和矛盾激化的结果，如领导人的下台、政府的重组等。

常用词汇

regime 政体，政权，政权制度
depose 免职，废除
cabinet 内阁
oust 驱逐，剥夺（权力）
factional 派系的，小派别的
exile 放逐，流放（者）
ruling party 执政党
overthrow 推翻，打倒
opposition 反对派
deportation 驱逐出境
hardliner 强硬路线派
repatriate 遣返
centrist 中立派（议员）
asylum 政治避难权；庇护所
left wing 左翼
amnesty（尤指对政治犯的）特赦

dissident 持不同政见者
dereliction of duty 渎职
caucus（政党的）领导人秘密会议
accountability 问责性
briefing 简报会
veto 否决
coalition government 联合政府
vote down 投票反对
reshuffle（政府）改组
impeach 弹劾
resign 辞职
compromise 妥协，折中
leave the office 辞职
concession 让步
abdicate 退位，放弃（职位，权力）
reconcile 和解

五、示威抗议

常见的考点：游行示威的原因、形式、地点、时间、人数；与警察冲突情况、伤亡和逮捕人数以及事件的发展方向，如谈判条件和谈判结果。

常用词汇

demonstration 示威
quell 镇压
hunger strike 绝食抗议
rally（群众性）集会

slogan 标语
sit-in 静坐示威
commemorate 纪念

六、暴力动乱

常见的考点：引发暴力和动乱的原因，事件发生的导火索及事件进展和结果，伤亡人数，损害程度以及社会反应和国际社会的反响等。

常用词汇

riot 暴动
repression 镇压
coup 政变
seal off 封锁
strife-ridden 冲突激烈的
cordon off 用警戒线围住
turmoil 骚动，混乱
curfew 宵禁
foment 煽动
barricade 设路障
chaos 混乱

checkpoint 检查站
bloodshed 流血；杀戮
teargas 催泪弹
loot 掠夺
apprehend 逮捕
loyalist 维护现有政权者
in custody 被关押，在拘禁中
insurgent 叛乱分子
detain 拘留
riot police 防暴警察

七、恐怖主义

常见的考点：恐怖事件发生的时间、地点、形式、政治目的及人员伤亡的情况；是否有组织声称对事件负责；恐怖主义的主要形式有劫机、绑架人质、暗杀、纵火、制造爆炸等。

常用词汇

anarchist 无政府主义者
aboriginal 土著居民的，土著的
activist 激进主义分子
serial bombing 连环爆炸
extremist 极端主义者
suicide bombing 自杀性爆炸
separatist 分离主义者
plastic explosive 塑胶炸药
nationalist 国家主义者，民族主义者
dynamite 炸药
fanatic 狂热者，盲信者
letter bomb 邮包炸弹
radical 激进分子
detonate 引爆
remnant 残余部分
go off 爆炸
affiliated 分支的，附属的
blast 爆炸，冲击波

provoke 挑拨，煽动
bomb-disposal expert 拆弹专家
instigate 鼓动，挑唆
defuse 去掉……的雷管；拆除炸弹
anti-American sentiment 反美情绪
char 烧焦
spiritual leader 精神领袖
remains 残骸
Koran《古兰经》(伊斯兰教经典)
vulnerable 易受攻击的
cleric 教会圣职人员
assassination 刺杀，暗杀
fundamentalist 宗教激进主义者
kidnapping 绑架
theocratic 神权的，神权政治的
hostage-taker 扣押人质者
secular 非宗教的，世俗的
hijack 劫持

synagogue 犹太教会堂
ambush 埋伏，伏击
mosque 清真寺
shrine 圣地
anthrax spores 炭疽孢子

ethnic minority 少数民族
claim the responsibility for 宣称对……负责
tribal 部族的
deny the charge 否认指控

常见的恐怖组织
Taliban 塔利班
Islamic Resistance Movement（Hamas）伊斯兰抵抗运动(简称哈马斯)
Basque separatist group（ETA）巴斯克分裂主义组织(简称艾塔)
al-Qaida 基地组织
Islamic Jihad Movement in Palestine 巴勒斯坦伊斯兰圣战运动
Hezbollah 真主党

▶▶▶ 八、军事行动

常见的考点：交战双方人数、交战时间、地点和方式、伤亡人数、现场损害程度等。
常用词汇

weapons of mass destruction 大规模杀伤性武器
drill 军事操练
biochemical weapons 生化武器
garrison 守卫，驻防
arsenal 兵工厂，军械库
station 驻扎，配置
shell 炮弹
headquarters 司令部，指挥部
ammunition 军火，弹药
base 基地
cruise missile 巡航导弹
outpost 前哨
ballistic missile 弹道导弹
stronghold 要塞，据点
siege 包围，围攻
grenade 手榴弹
bombard 炮击，轰炸
mine 地雷
storm 猛攻
artillery 炮兵部队
assault 攻击
patrol 巡逻队

assail 攻击
armored vehicle 装甲车
intercept 阻截
personnel carrier 运兵车
snipe 狙击
helicopter 直升机
air strike 空袭
ground troops 地面部队
raid 奇袭
paratrooper 伞兵
gun down 枪杀
armed forces 武装部队
exchange fire 交火
corps（医务、军械、通信等兵种名称）队
shootout 交火
coast guards 海岸警卫队
sporadic shots 零星战斗
military police 宪兵
retaliation 报复，报仇
coalition troops 联合部队
reinforcement 援军
multinational forces 多国部队
withdraw 撤离

international peace-keeper 国际维和部队
dissolve 解散(军队)
occupation forces 占领军
disband 解散(军队)
militant 武装分子
disengagement 脱离
militia 民兵
disarmament 裁军
warlord 军阀
demilitarize 解除武装,废除军备
dictator 独裁者
truce 休战,休战协定
guerrilla 游击队
ceasefire 停火
recruit 新兵
power transfer 权力的移交
veteran 老兵
prisoner swap 交换战俘

civilian 平民
caretaker government 临时政府
military operation 军事行动
interim transitional government 临时过渡政府
deployment 部署
air space 领空
mobilize 动员(军队)
territory 领土
authorize 授权,批准
arms inspection 武器核查
ally 结盟
military intelligence 军事情报
escalate (战争)升级
morale 士气
dispatch 派遣(军队)
logistic 后勤的
maneuver 调遣,演习

九、核武问题

核问题是全球关注的问题,包括两个方面。一方面,旨在推动防止核军备竞赛的国际条约(如《核不扩散条约》)得到国际社会的认同;另一方面,关注核试验、核技术泄密事件等威胁国际安全的问题。

常用词汇

disablement 去功能化
nuclear weapons 核武器
nuclear proliferation 核扩散
dismantle 拆除

weakened uranium weapons 贫铀武器
nuclear warhead 核弹头
nuclear test 核试验
black market 黑市

十、天灾人祸

常见的考点:地震、飓风、海啸、火山爆发、洪水、山体滑坡等自然灾害;煤气泄漏、爆炸、坠机、列车出轨、沉船等事故;伤亡人数、受灾范围、出事时间、出事地点、事故原因、救援措施等。

常用词汇

earthquake 地震
volcano eruption 火山爆发
flood 洪灾
drought 旱灾
tsunami 海啸

hurricane 飓风
typhoon 台风
tornado 龙卷风
tropical storm 热带风暴
sandstorm 沙尘暴

snowstorm 暴风雪
blizzard 暴风雪
mudslide 泥石流
landslide 滑坡
landslip 滑坡，塌方
forest fire 森林火灾
death toll 死亡人数
humanitarian 人道主义者
rescue 援救，营救
relief 救济
rescuer 救助者
aid worker 救援人员
natural calamity 自然灾害
strike 侵袭，爆发
survivor 幸存者
claim-(life) 夺走……生命
casualty 伤亡人员
homeless 无家可归的

refugee 难民
victim 受害者，遇难者
famine 饥荒
afflicted district 受灾地区
meltdown 灾难性事件
bereaved 丧失亲人者
invalid 病弱者
capsize （特指船）倾覆
fuel leak 燃油泄漏
shipwreck 船只失事，海难
ferry accident 渡船事故
salvage 海上救助，打捞
derailment 出轨
evacuation 撤离，疏散
collision 碰撞
collide 碰撞；冲突
paralyze 使瘫痪

▶▶▶ 十一、经济与商业

常见的考点：经济形势、经济繁荣或衰退的原因；经济不景气所引起的其他问题，如失业率增加、物价上涨、通货膨胀率上升等；各国进出口商品贸易以及贸易纠纷；金融和股票市场形势，汇率变化，股价涨跌，黄金和油价的波动等；某些支柱产业的发展状况，如汽车业、钢铁业、电信业和IT业等；各种问题相关的数字和百分比，如GDP数值、经济增长率、贸易额、营业额、汇率、股价、油价等。

常用词汇

recession 经济衰退，不景气
automaker 汽车造商
fiscal year〈美〉财政年度
telecommunications 电信业
reserve 储备金
steel industry 钢铁工业
revenue 收入，国家的收入，税收
market （有组织地、大规模地）销售
budget 预算
securities 证券
deficit 赤字
bond 债券
in the red 赤字，亏损

share 股票，股份
insolvent 破产的
deflation 通货紧缩
euro 欧元
protectionism 贸易保护主义
sponsor 赞助
trade barrier 贸易壁垒
multinational 跨国公司
tariff 关税
corporate bankruptcy 公司破产
dump 倾销
yen 日元
quota 配额

ounce 盎司
tertiary industry 第三产业
barrel （原油）桶
NASDAQ index 纳斯达克指数
Dow-Jones industrial average 道琼斯工业平均指数
in the black 盈余
exchange rate 汇率
inflation 通货膨胀

十二、司法审判

常见的考点：严重的刑事犯罪、经济犯罪，特别是政治性案件，如政治丑闻、犯下战争罪的前国家领导人等。案件的当事人、证据、审判过程、定罪、引渡、量刑、社会反响等。

常用词汇

extradition 引渡
indictment 控告，起诉
indict 起诉，控告
convict 证明有罪
Supreme Court 最高法院
wiretap 搭线窃听，窃听或偷录
court martial 军事法庭
lawmaker 立法者
jurisdictional 司法的
sue 提出诉讼
penal code 刑法典
lawsuit 诉讼（非刑事案件）
civil law 民法
confession 坦白，承认
amendment 修正案
denial 否认
draft 起草
session 开庭，开庭期
verdict （陪审团的）裁决
enact 制定法律，颁布
trial 审判，审讯
legitimize 使合法
judge 法官
ban 禁止
repeal 废止，撤销
jury 陪审团
unconstitutional 违宪的
defendant 被告
prosecutor 原告；起诉人；检察官

plaintiff 原告
armed robbery 武装抢劫
arson 纵火
attorney 律师
drug trafficking 贩毒
testimony 证词
fraudulency 欺诈，诈骗
capital punishment 死刑
expulsion 逐出，开除
larceny 盗窃罪
electrocution 电刑
smuggling 走私
extradite 引渡
treason 叛国罪
appeal 上诉
war crime 战争罪
bail 保释，保释金
bribery 受贿；行贿
parole 假释
corruption an 腐败
perjury 伪誓，伪证
embezzlement 贪污
loophole 漏洞
culprit 歹徒，逃犯
obstruct justice 阻挠司法
outlaw 犯人
tamper with a witness 收买证人
homicide 杀人，杀人者
prisoner abuse 虐囚

suspect 嫌疑犯
sex humiliation 性侮辱
law enforcement 执法

torture 拷问
lie detector 测谎仪
inmate（监狱）同室者

十三、卫生保健

常见的考点：大规模瘟疫爆发，如疯牛病、非典、禽流感、口蹄疫等；患病人数及年龄、感染地区分布、疾病的死亡率、传染途径、预防和治疗措施等。

常用词汇

outbreak （疾病的）突然发生
susceptible 易得病的人
mad cow disease 疯牛病
symptom 症状
hoof-and-mouth disease 口蹄疫
mortality rate 死亡率
west Nile virus 西尼罗河病毒
precaution 预防措施
bird flu 禽流感
quarantine 检疫，隔离
epidemic 流行病
vaccination 接种疫苗
complication 并发症
immunization 免疫
transmit 传染

slaughter 屠宰（动物）
contract 感染（疾病）
cull 有选择地屠宰
-borne 由……携带的，如：water-borne diseases 由水传染的疾病；air-borne diseases 由空气传染的疾病
serum 血清
incidence 发生率
eradicate 根除
high-risk areas 高危地区
cholera 霍乱
malaria 疟疾
tuberculosis（TB）肺结核
cancer 癌症
AIDS 艾滋病

十四、难民问题

常见的考点：产生难民的原因、难民的数量和生存情况、难民的收容和遣返问题、难民问题引发的国际争端以及人道主义危机。

常用词汇

refugee camp 难民营
genocide 种族大屠杀
sanctuary 庇护所

humanitarian aid 人道主义援助
holocaust 大屠杀

十五、新闻中常见的地名、组织和政府机构

常用词汇

1. 新闻中常见的地名

Cuba 古巴
Cuban 古巴的，古巴人
Bangladesh 孟加拉国
Indonesia 印度尼西亚

Indonesian 印度尼西亚人；印度尼西亚的
Timor-Leste 东帝汶
Bali 巴厘岛

Bulgaria 保加利亚
Romania 罗马尼亚
Israeli 以色列的；以色列人
Israel 以色列
Gaza 加沙
Palestinian 巴勒斯坦（人）的；巴勒斯坦人
Somalia 索马里
Mediterranean Sea 地中海
Libya 利比亚
Mexican 墨西哥人；墨西哥的
Argentina 阿根廷
Argentine 阿根廷人阿根廷的
Zimbabwe 津巴布韦
Afghanistan 阿富汗
Mongolia 蒙古
Luxembourg 卢森堡
Iran 伊朗

Iraq 伊拉克
Qatar 卡塔尔
Lebanon 黎巴嫩
Pakistan 巴基斯坦
Pakistani 巴基斯坦人；巴基斯坦的
Northern Ireland 北爱尔兰
Nigeria 尼日利亚
Adriatic Sea 亚得里亚海
Albania 阿尔巴尼亚
Albanian 阿尔巴尼亚人；阿尔巴尼亚的
Kosovo 科索沃
Malaysian 马来西亚的；马来西亚人
Columbia （美国的）哥伦比亚
Haitian 海地的；海地人
Serbia 塞尔维亚
Serb 塞尔维亚人；塞尔维亚的
Danube 多瑙河
Yugoslavia 南斯拉夫

2. 常见的联合国机构、国际性组织及区域性组织

General Assembly of the United Nations 联合国大会

United Nations Security Council (UNSC) 联合国安理会

United Nations High Commissioner for Refugees (UNHCR, Short for Refugee Agency) 联合国难民事务高级专员办事处,简称联合国难民署

United Nations Children's Fund (UNICEF) 联合国儿童基金会

United Nations Development Programme (UNDP) 联合国开发计划署

United Nations Educational, Scientific and Cultural Organization (UNESCO) 联合国教育、科学及文化组织,简称联合国教科文组织

Food and Agriculture Organization (FAO) 联合国粮食及农业组织

International Court of Justice (ICJ) 国际法院

International Atomic Energy Agency (IAEA) 国际原子能机构

International Monetary Fund (IMF) 国际货币基金组织

World Health Organization (WHO) 世界卫生组织

World Trade Organization (WTO) 世界贸易组织

International Committee of Red Cross (ICRC) 红十字国际委员会

African National Congress (ANC) 非洲人国民大会

Group of Seven (G7) 七国集团

North Atlantic Treaty Organization (NATO) 北大西洋公约组织

Organization of Petroleum Exporting Countries (OPEC) 石油输出国组织

National Aeronautics and Space Administration (NASA) 美国国家航空航天局
Central Intelligence Agency (CIA) 中央情报局
Federal Bureau of Investigation (FBI) 联邦调查局
Federal Reserve Bank (The Fed) 美国联邦储备银行
Coalition Provisional Authority (CPA) 联盟驻伊拉克临时管理委员会
Asia-Pacific Economic Cooperation (APEC) 亚太经济合作组织

3. 政府主要行政职称、机构、党派、宗教派别名称
Upper House 上议院
Lower House 下议院
Senate (美国) 参议院
House of Representatives (美国) 众议院
House of Lords (英国) 国会上议院
House of Commons (英国) 国会下议院
State Department 国务院
Secretary of State 国务卿
National Security Advisor 国家安全顾问
Prime Minister 总理,首相
Chancellor (德国) 总理
Foreign Minister 外交部部长
Defense Secretary 国防部部长
Interior Minister 内政部部长
Finance Minister 财政部部长
the Treasury Secretary 财政部部长
the Chancellor of Exchequer (英国) 财政大臣
the Republican Party (美国) 共和党
the Democratic Party (美国) 民主党
Iraqi Shiite 伊拉克的什叶派
Iraqi Sunni 伊拉克的逊尼派

References
参考文献

[1] Connie Shoemaker, Susan Polycarpou. Inside the News: A Reading Text for Students of English[M]. Boston: Heinle & Heinle Publishers, 2001.

[2] Mina Rastegar, Ehsan Mehrabi Kermani, Massoud Khabir. The Relationship between Metacognitive Reading Strategies Use and Reading Comprehension Achievement of EFL Learners[J]. Open Journal of Modern Linguistics, 2017(7).

[3] Yomana Chandran, Parilah M. Shah. Identifying Learners' Difficulties in ESL Reading Comprehension[J]. Creative Education, 2019(10).

[4] 赖铮,霍健明."一带一路"视野下的东盟十国:文化教育与商业机遇[M].厦门:厦门大学出版社,2019.

[5] 汤燕瑜,邬跃生.东盟国家社会与文化[M].苏州:苏州大学出版社,2009.

[6] 张健.新闻英语文体与范文评析[M].上海:上海外语教育出版社,2004.

[7] 张健.报刊英语研究[M].上海:上海外语教育出版社,2007.

[8] 夏廷德,马志波.实用新闻英语翻译[M].北京:对外经济贸易大学出版社,2010.

References
参考文献